THE LITTLE BLACK BOOK OF
BUDGETS AND
FORECASTS

THE LITTLE BLACK BOOK OF BUDGETS AND FORECASTS

Michael C. Thomsett

amacom
American Management Association

This book is available at a special
discount when ordered in bulk quantities.
For information, contact Special Sales Department,
AMACOM, a division of American Management Association,
1601 Broadway, New York, NY 10019.

Library of Congress Cataloging-in-Publication Data

Thomsett, Michael C.
    The little black book of budgets and
forecasts.

    Includes index.
    1. Budget in business.   I. Title.
HG4028.B8T56   1988   658.1'54   87–47842
ISBN 0–8144–7692–0

Printing number

20   19   18   17   16

for
Linda

Preface

Budgeting is a process that every manager must eventually face. In some organizations, it is assumed that this is a strictly accounting function. And unfortunately, the entire budgeting process is often assigned to the accounting department. When this occurs, managers in other departments do not have the opportunity to use budgeting to manage, predict, and—to some extent—control the future.

It might be appropriate to control your organization's budget in one central location such as the corporate accounting department. However, each manager will ultimately be expected to answer when costs and expenses exceed an assumed level, or when income is well below a forecast. Correct budgeting enables you to set goals for financial results in your department, and for the organization at large. You can improve budgeting success by evaluating past budgets and their degree of accuracy. And ultimately, you will be able to select appropriate methods for estimating the future, meaning higher profits and improved perceptions by management of your value as a farsighted and capable employee.

Most organizations experience great difficulty in budgeting, notably during periods of rapid expansion. No one book can propose solutions to every possible situation, and our purpose is not to assume that budgeting and forecasting are simple procedures. This book does offer guidelines, however, both for the overall approach to budgeting that will help you master the process and for specific solutions to common problems we all face.

Budgets might be developed as a means for proper control, or they might be imposed on you from above. In either case, you will make the most of the task at hand by keeping in mind that the purpose of doing a budget is to estimate. Don't think of budgeting as something that you must do only to comply with an annual ritual. Think of it as a way to take control of your immediate environment, to master the financial aspects of your job and department, and to solve problems *before* they become critical.

The *Little Black Book* series attempts to address problems such as those encountered by all preparers of budgets and forecasts. This is accomplished by presenting problems that arise in most organizations and showing how those problems can best be solved. This book and the other books in the series do not answer every question you will have on a topic. Far from it. They provide guidelines for the most practical ways to approach problems and develop solutions. They show by example how to set priorities, improve management's perception of your work and its quality, and simplify your professional life.

M.C.T.

Contents

Introduction

We can lick gravity, but sometimes the paperwork is overwhelming.

— Werner Von Braun

Paperwork. That's how many people view the budgeting process, and for good reason. At one bank holding company, the year-end project was so complicated that it wasn't even presented until the close of the first quarter. By that time, the actual results for the first three months were known, so the budget was predictably accurate. When the committee chairman was asked whether the second quarter would turn out as well, he replied, "Yes, but only if we have time to finish up the revised budget by then."

There are sound reasons for predicting future levels of income, costs, and expenses, and for attempting to anticipate cash flow. Budgeting can be more than an exercise in paperwork, and more than a time-consuming and arbitrary function that most employees dread at the end of the year. Properly done and used, budgeting can and should increase profits, reduce unnecessary spending, and clearly define how immediate steps can be taken to expand markets.

Many well-intentioned budgeting procedures achieve only part of the objective: The process is put into place. However, the company will not derive benefits from an empty procedure. Only by following through and taking action on the information created in the budgeting process will it become a profit center.

Most of us have experienced the tightening of the budget. Management points to lower profits or adverse market conditions as a reason to cut expenses or to defer hiring new staff members until conditions change. Equally important but more often ignored is the need for careful control when volume and profits are high. Many companies make lower profits during times of growth—often because they do not control spending. At those times, the exercise of mandated restraints is not only smart management. It is a necessary component of growth.

This little black book proposes a specific method for the preparation and use of budgets and forecasts. All of the steps are explained with examples, from the initial justification of budgeting as a process, through documenting of assumptions, income, expense and cash flow reports, presentations to management, and turning the budget into a source for profits. Each chapter concludes with exercises for the development of your own budgeting skills. Solutions and alternatives are included in appendix A.

In some organizations, the terms "forecast," "budget," and "projection" are used interchangeably. In this book these terms are used as follows: A forecast pertains to income, a budget is for expenses, and a projection is for future cash flow. The collective process is called "budgeting." A complete list of budgeting terms appears in chapter 1.

Budgeting has both a concept and a reality. The real-life problems you face are vastly different from the mere theory of how budgets should work. You're probably expected to develop detailed budgets, only to have them changed arbitrarily by someone above you. The budget must be produced quickly under great pressure, often at a time of the year when you're under deadline on other things, too. And you probably have little say in the running of the whole procedure. With this book, you'll learn how to deal with these realities by:

■ Developing a sound procedure that both justifies your budget and helps improve your techniques.

■ Suggesting useful ideas to management to improve the company's internal budgeting procedure.

■ Dealing with realities that contradict sound procedures for researching and developing a budget.

As your own little black book, this volume will be your personal outline for effective and successful budgeting. It will give you alternatives, enable you to suggest improvements in your own company's procedures, and will become a valuable reference. You'll also learn how to create foolproof documentation for the assumptions that go into the actual numbers—conclusions that might otherwise seem arbitrary. You may want to keep this book on your person at all times, thinking of it as your "secret weapon." As fellow employees see the change in your effectiveness, they might be tempted to rifle through your desk in order to learn your secrets. Guard them well.

1

Why Budgets Fail

One half of the world cannot understand the pleasures of the other.

—Jane Austen

The procedures in one corporation called for the preparation of a monthly forecast on the first Friday of every month. The only time the report had been questioned was the month that one page had been put in upside down. So the accounting manager did not review what his staff put in the report, but insisted that each copy be "paginated" and checked to make certain that it was in the right order and that no pages were put in incorrectly. He reasoned, "As long as it looks right, no one will question it."

Ask anyone in your company, "What's the purpose of budgeting?" The answer will usually be that it gives management an idea of how well income goals are being met, whether or not expenses are in line with predicted levels, and how well controls are working. But in fact, budgeting is often an ineffective procedure, improperly used and involving a great deal of arbitrary and time-consuming effort.

Next, ask what kinds of actions are taken when budgets vary from the predicted course. In most cases, this question will mystify others. All too often, the budgeting process becomes the end in itself, and its purpose is lost in the deadlines and pressure to get it done.

Even with the best theories in hand, you cannot change the way your company is managed without presenting good, solid ideas. You have to be aware of the problems you face, not just in building an accurate prediction of the future, but in dealing with the four common reasons why budgets fail:

1. Manipulation. You spend hours coming up with a realistic budget, only to have it cut in review. Or during the year, journal entries are made to defer expenses that would cause a variance; or expenses are miscoded by account or department.
2. Incomplete variance explanations. Variances should be analyzed and explained in a monthly report. All too often, no report is done, or its explanations give the reader no valid information on which to act.
3. Blaming or distorting. Budgets may be used as political rather than control tools. This distortion harms everyone. The company has no way to measure its effectiveness, and the employees who must work with the budget spend a great deal of time for nothing of value.
4. Lack of recommendations or action. Unfortunately, most managers view a variance as an opportunity only for identifying a problem, and they don't go a step further to recommend a solution. It's true that top managers won't always respond favorably to solutions recommended on a budget report. However, with *no* recommendations before them, they *can't* respond and *your* role in the process of change is severely diminished.

MANIPULATING NUMBERS

"There's really nothing that I can do," is a popular rationale for not following up on information derived from comparing budgets to actual results. But at the same time, top management demands explanations for variances, even from individuals who did not prepare the budget itself.

Rather than presenting a constructive approach, budget reports often just show an "acceptable" explanation for deficiencies. In some companies, adjustments are made by way of journal entry—the sole motive being to eliminate an unfavorable variance and make the report more "in line" with the forecast.

In one company, the first quarter's printing expenses were nearly 30% above budget, and a variance of $6,500 had to be explained. But rather than looking for flaws in the budget or control problems in the expense itself, a journal entry was prepared deferring the $6,500, with the explanation, "To defer expenses properly belonging in future periods."

Reducing the variance makes the expense appear to be in line. An explanation is no longer needed, although the deferral must be absorbed at some point in the future. But this solution to one problem creates a much greater problem. Manipulation of the financial report to suit a budget gives management a false summary of status.

In another company, income fell below the forecast. When it came time to prepare a monthly budget report, a journal entry was prepared to book additional income. It reduced a 22% unfavorable variance down to about 7%. The explanation on the journal was, "To record estimated income earned in June and expected to be received in July."

The explanation of the 7% variance read:

> The unfavorable variance is 7.0% of the forecast income level. This is expected to be absorbed during the summer months.

That's a reassuring explanation. The percentage is not great, and it will probably disappear later on. But manipulating numbers leaves the underlying problems unrevealed and unexplored. So management receives no real, useful information.

Altering actual results to comply with the budget is counter to the purpose of budgeting but is a common practice. This is a sign that the company's leadership has placed too much emphasis on "correct" budgets and too little on valid control procedures and positive action. While the pressure from management to correct variances in the budget is often unavoidable, there *are* conservative ways to explain variances without putting your—or anyone else's—job on the line.

In one organization, for example, the manager of customer service prepared a budget report for salaries and wages in her own department, which included 11 employees. The actual figures exceeded budget by more than 20%. Nine months before, when the budget was prepared, she had requested additional staffing, which was refused. And over the last year she had asked for updated support systems. All of her requests were turned down. Before the budget meeting, her manager warned her to be prepared for a lot of criticism about the over-budget condition. Her explanation read:

1. Comparison.

    Salaries and wages, 9 months:
Year-to-date	$207,130
Forecast	$172,400
Variance	$ (34,730)
% Variance	(20.1%)

2. Explanation. The original budget for salaries and wages was based on the assumption that current staff levels were adequate for workloads projected into this year.

    The volume in calls and letters from customers has increased from an average last year of 1,300 per month to more than 1,900, growth of 46%. The unfavorable variance was caused by overtime worked by the department's staff.

3. Analysis. The negative trend will continue given present staff levels. New accounts and the volume of sales have more than doubled from the same period last year.

    The present budget level is unrealistic, and the level of growth in new accounts and gross volume was not anticipated when the budget was prepared.

4. Recommendations. Our present budget does not allow for the substantial growth in sales or customers. Accordingly, the following recommendations are offered:
    1. Revise the department's salaries and wages budget in line with current information about volume.
    2. Authorize the hiring of two additional customer service representatives, to eliminate costly overtime.
    3. Review customer service procedures and determine whether more efficient systems will help reduce the time required to respond to customer requests.

The unfavorable variance was predictable. The manager knew nearly a full year before that her budget was inadequate to meet a growing demand. But note that while the report clearly identifies the problem and offers solutions it does not blame others.

Management is certainly aware of how this problem developed, as it had refused the request for more staff and updated support systems. But if the report had cited a management failure it would certainly fail in objectivity and usefulness.

From the kind of thorough analysis and conclusion presented by this manager, top management now has the choice: Either live with the unfavorable variance, or revise the budget and take appropriate action to save money in the future.

INCOMPLETE VARIANCE EXPLANATIONS

Management does, indeed, look for information. That's why a variance report is a crucial part of the budgeting process. But most "explanations" give nothing of value to a reviewer. For example, the expense for dues and subscriptions shows a 9% unfavorable variance. Typical explanations might read:

> Expenses exceeded budget by 9%.

> The unfavorable variance was caused by timing differences; this will be offset in future months.

> The variance was caused by expenses in excess of those anticipated at the time the budget was prepared.

All of these statements have one thing in common: They don't say anything. The first statement merely repeats the obvious. The second makes a broad assertion without any support. And the third also states the obvious. For someone interested in taking action in response to discovered problems in the budget, these explanations are useless.

A variance explanation has to explain the underlying causes of variances. Either the budget did not include items that it should have, or there is a lack of control. A possible explanation:

> The 9% variance is due to three major causes. (1) Subscriptions were taken to several publications not included in the budget; (2) the company joined an organization and paid $1,100 in dues, also not in the budget; and (3) there is no internal procedure for preapproval of dues and subscriptions.

In this example, specific reasons are given for the unfavorable variance. Now management has information that enables it to act. The decision could be made, for example, to improve budgeting procedures to include every possible item. It may also decide to effect a new policy requiring preapproval of dues and subscriptions.

BLAMING OR DISTORTING

The budget is only an estimate, a standard against which you and other employees can measure results. Blame should not be assigned for variances; the energy should be put into identifying errors or conditions that caused that variance (or problem in the budget) and then taking the right action.

In your company you may discover that each individual claims someone else is responsible for actions. Middle managers may assume that top management will decide when to take corrective action. And top management may assume that middle managers and supervisors should enact controls, or at least prepare accurate and dependable budgets.

The budgeting procedure in one offset printing company called for monthly reports and variance explanations. The president insisted on identification of precise causes for all unfavorable conditions. Postage expenses were a constant problem, and identifying the actual cause proved a real challenge. The office manager blamed the sales department; the sales people insisted the clerical staff was inefficient; and the clerical employees said they only responded to daily pressures. The truth was that cooperation would have enabled better planning of mailings (thus reducing the frequency of overnight and special deliveries). But it took many months to arrive at this basic truth and to develop new procedures. Why? Because rather than dealing with the problem, everyone was busy pointing the finger at someone else.

When management places too much pressure on employees to explain a problem, it creates an opportunity for responses like those in the offset printing company. If the emphasis is placed on blame, solutions will be elusive. The emphasis should be on solving the problem, whatever it is, rather than on finding out who made a mistake.

Budgets can also be used as weapons in internal political conflicts. The marketing manager in a national insurance agency had many disagreements with the accounting department. When travel and entertainment expenses exceeded the budget by 20%, he explained:

> The variance is caused by incorrect budget preparation, and by improper coding of administrative travel expenses to the marketing department.

This type of explanation contributes nothing to the solutions management will seek in attempting to control expense levels. Rather, it will only escalate the conflict, prevent communication and agreement, and make it more difficult to work together. The "other side" must then respond with a defense or a counterclaim. The result: Nothing positive comes from the exchange and the problem remains (see "Action Ideas").

Action Ideas: Eliminating Political Conflict

Reduce the effects of political misuse of the budgeting and forecasting process with these ideas:

1. Suggest to management that final budgets be prepared by a committee representing several different departments, subject to review by everyone affected.
2. Also suggest that variances be explained by a manager who prepared the budget.
3. Prepare complete documentation for all forecast and budget assumptions, and be ready to explain how numbers were developed.
4. Avoid blaming variances on other departments or individuals. Concentrate on constructive ideas for reversing negative trends.
5. Identify the causes of variances and avoid repeating mistakes in future budgets.
6. When mistakes are found in the budget itself, suggest a revision rather than assigning blame.

LACK OF RECOMMENDATIONS OR ACTIONS

Effective reports have two important features. The first is identification of the cause of the problem. Is it due to incomplete budgeting, unanticipated conditions in the market, lack of control or monitoring, or a combination of these? The second is recommendations for action.

The person preparing a budget report is rarely in the position to directly correct a trend. But that person can take steps to make the report valuable to management, whether it is a companywide or a departmental budget.

Can you make recommendations to management to correct a negative trend? Or, if you supervise others who prepare budget reports, can you train them to analyze and present facts? Yes you can! Of course, risk always accompanies suggesting action beyond the minimum expected response. But as a rule, being outspoken can only backfire if ideas cannot be supported with fact. And supported ideas must be viewed as they are intended—as constructive and well-motivated recommendations.

For example, in a corporation that publishes a daily newspaper, the accounting manager acknowledged that revenues from advertising were substantially lower than the forecast levels. His budget report consisted only of a comparison between actual and forecast amounts, without explanation or suggestions for action.

An effective budget report would have contained several elements:

1. A comparison between actual and forecast. Anyone reviewing the report should be able to see at a glance exactly where variances have occurred and their significance. The degree of variance is often expressed both in dollar amount and percentage (comparing the variance to the budgeted amount). For example:

    Advertising revenue, 4 months:

Year-to-date	$214,935	
Forecast	310,000	
Variance	$ (95,065)	(30.7%)

2. An explanation of causes, which can be given only when the budget is well documented and its assumptions and their flaws can be identified. For example, if the budget is prepared as a percentage increase over last year's numbers (a common technique) it is impossible to identify why the variance exists. But a complete and comprehensive analysis of factors affecting the budget supports the explanation. No one is expected to hit an expense on the nose, nor is that the purpose of budgeting. But the budget should point to causes and trends, in order to be truly valuable. For example:

    Income forecasts were based on the assumption that average advertising revenues would increase over levels in the prior year by 3% per month. However, average revenues from recurring accounts have remained at the same level as during the previous year; and 13 major accounts no longer place business with us.

3. Analysis. It may be that revenues are falling behind schedule because of outside influences or economic conditions or loss of a major account. Or due to timing, receipts may be booked in the following month. Examining the account in line with original assumptions makes the problems evident, either because of failures in the assumptions or factors influencing actual results.

   It is not realistic to expect the unfavorable variance to reverse itself without additional marketing efforts. The forecast did not anticipate losing major accounts, which occurred because a competing daily paper offered lower rates.

4. Recommendations. A valuable budget report must suggest corrective actions. Even an employee who cannot dictate corrective actions can present alternatives. It is then up to management to execute appropriate actions, but it can only do so when it is given information as in this sample:

   Even if management decides to institute aggressive marketing for advertising revenues, the effects of that effort will not be reflected on the books for several months. The following steps are proposed:

   1. Revise advertising income forecasts in view of lost accounts.
   2. Review the current rate structure and consider adjustments in line with the competition.
   3. Create a current year marketing and sales plan in view of the competition for accounts, including volume goals for account managers.

Note that this report explores and explains the variance in depth, then gives specific recommendations. Management now has a clear choice. Presenting an accurate summary of status is only the beginning, the definition of a problem. If a report doesn't go beyond this and give ideas to management, it fails.

These elements, used consistently, will help make budgets useful and effective. But the problem of communicating and then resolving budget problems is compounded by the terminology problem. Help clarify definitions in your company. "Budgeting Terminology" presents a listing of suggested words and their meanings.

Your experience as a participant in the budgeting process can be a satisfying one—but only if you are able to control it, and to make it a tool for anticipating the future, preparing for it, and creating it.

That may seem too high an ideal for anyone who has suffered through the mechanisms of budgets and endless revisions. But the following chapters show how budgeting can be controlled and turned into a vehicle for more effective reporting and greater profits.

Budgeting Terminology

The following terminology appears in this book. These words may have different meanings in your company, or might be used interchangeably in some cases.

Assumption: the facts or beliefs that are used to justify estimates used in the budget.

Assumption base: the premise for developing an assumption. For example, one expense account might be estimated on the basis of the number of employees, and another tied directly to revenues.

Budget: (1) in the broad sense, "budget" refers to the entire process of estimating future revenues, expenses, and cash flow; (2) specifically, the budget is an estimate of future expense levels.

Forecast: an estimate of future revenues the company will earn and receive.

Projection: an estimate of future levels of cash available to the organization.

Proposal: a written suggestion to management, using facts and statistics, notably relating to forecasts and budgets.

Source: information used in development of assumptions. For example, historical information or interviews with other managers can be sources for an expense account assumption. And a marketing expansion plan can be referred to as a source for developing an income forecast.

WORK PROJECT

1. You are instructed to prepare this year's budget for printing expenses at 10% above last year's level. What problems might you expect to encounter in explaining variances? When would this method be appropriate?

2. You assign an employee the task of developing a budget for the coming year's telephone expenses. How would you instruct him to justify his numbers?

3. You are coordinating the budget for several other departments. The marketing manager has increased all expenses for travel, entertainment, and telephone, even though one of seven field offices has been closed. How would you suggest a revision?

2

Making Budgets Succeed

There cannot be a crisis next week. My schedule is already full.

—Henry Kissinger

The vice president of administration was generally pleased with the current year's budget. For the most part, variances were minor and it appeared that an accurate budgeting job had been done. The one exception was in the travel and entertainment expense account, where unfavorable variances were chronic. When he asked for ideas, one manager stated, "It would be quite a task to come up with a way to predict and control the future."

Exactly. It is quite a task to create and use an effective budget. But it is possible to control the future to the extent that income, costs, expenses, and cash flow are predictable.

SEGMENTS OF THE COMPLETE BUDGET

Properly devised predictions make the difference between mundane routines and effective management tools. This principle applies differently in each of the three segments of the complete budget, income forecasting, expense budgets, and cash flow projections:

1. Income forecasting. Estimating future revenues guides the company in several ways. Being aware of limits directly affects the ability to commit funds for expansion, for example. And an income forecast should also be used to set goals. An aggressive but realistic estimate of revenues can be translated into individual quotas, or can show marketing management the level of new recruitment that will be needed to meet those revenue standards.
2. Expense budgets. The forecast also dictates the appropriate levels of many expense categories. For example, a vastly higher level of volume will require a greater commitment to travel, telephone, administrative support staff salaries, and other variable expenses. Even fixed expenses can be affected. If greater volume means expansion of clerical staff, larger facilities will be needed—thus, a higher rent expense.

   Organizations prepare expense budgets to avoid excessive spending. This is equally important in environments of growth and of recession. When income is down, the company cannot afford to spend money unnecessarily. And when income is up, expense controls tend to be relaxed. As a result, the company may earn a smaller margin of profit than it would in a well-controlled situation.
3. Cash flow projections. This is the most frequently ignored aspect of budgeting, but one of the most important. Profits are not the only objective in operating the company from year to year; cash must also be available. Several factors can adversely affect cash flow, including a growing level of accounts receivable, excessive investment in fixed assets, or too high a level of debt (requiring monthly repayments of principal and interest).

These three parts are inter-related and must be coordinated carefully. Otherwise, the entire budgeting experience falls short. Your experience as a participant in the budgeting process can be satisfying—but only if you can make the budget a tool for anticipating the future, preparing for it, and creating it.

A COMMON ATTITUDE
AN ENLIGHTENED POINT OF VIEW

One point of view is that budgeting is merely a bureaucratic process with little or no value. In many organizations, this is true, but only because the budgeting process is incomplete.

There's another way to view budgets. They exist and are justified because organizations can, in fact, use them to reach goals and minimize expenses, to anticipate and plan for periods when operating capital is low, and to build consistent profits. To achieve these intentions, follow the guidelines in "Checklist: Making the Process Effective."

Example: A financial services company devised a budget to expand its market from 14 to 47 states within one year. Because it is a regulated industry, the major hurdle was obtaining licensing approval, the requirements for which varied considerably from state to state. The initial marketing plan estimated the legal and registration fees and allowed for a reasonable level of travel and recruitment costs. But the plan had flaws.

Checklist: Making the Process Effective

1. Place emphasis on assumptions, recognizing that all items—income, costs, expenses, and cash flow—have logical assumption bases.
2. Do not budget for a preconceived level of sales or profits.
3. Recognize the absolute relationship between income volume and certain classifications of general expenses.
4. Involve all departments in the budgeting process while controlling the preparation phase in one central department or committee.
5. Resist arbitrary budgeting, instead setting a standard for logical and intelligent assumptions.
6. Prepare monthly reports comparing actual to budgets, emphasizing significant variances.
7. Make specific recommendations for action that should be taken in response to the revelations of the budget report.
8. Encourage the development of written budget standards and procedures within your department and company.

A careful analysis of the projected budget was undertaken, based not only on the cost of becoming licensed in remote locations but also on the expectation of profit. Sparsely populated states would not generate volume justified by the higher cost of operating remote branch offices. Management acknowledged that the greater the distance of a region from the home office, the higher the cost of operation . . . and the greater the cost of development.

The plan was modified substantially to focus not on becoming licensed in a majority of states, but to create a market in areas of concentrated population. The company depended on volume. And an analysis of past years revealed several relevant points:

1. Regions closer to the home state were more profitable over time, while remote regions tended to show smaller volume on a per-representative basis.
2. Rural areas were expensive to maintain and produced relatively small volumes. Urban areas were more profitable markets.
3. Regional economic conditions affected the market.

Perhaps most significant was the cash flow projection for the multistate development. Like all organizations, this firm had a finite level of cash available. Expanding as rapidly as had been planned would be dangerous. Upon review, management saw that a successful expansion plan would depend on methodical and controlled growth, rather than the idea to "go national" in one year.

The final plan put into place succeeded with the methodical approach. Over a three-year period, the company established specific regions. Once strength was established, those remote regions were expanded into subregions. As expansion crossed state lines, the company sought approval as part of natural growth, not just to create a presence.

This plan was based on the realities of cash flow limitations. It made no sense to risk regional expansion for its own sake without first considering the relative strength of different markets. The phases were distinct, and minimized risks:

—Phase 1—regional offices were created in identified urban centers.
—Phase 2—upon establishing a *profitable* operation in each region, the

company opened new offices in outlying suburban or smaller urban centers. Essential to this plan was that regional offices took charge of subregional development, relieving the remote home office from the high cost of working in unfamiliar and distant territory.

A contingency plan was included. If a region turned out to not be profitable, the company would pull back—rather than sinking yet more time and money into a failed venture.

Through analysis of cash flow and expense realities within the budgeting process, the marketing plan was taken from an impractical and risky idea into a controllable process.

The proper use of budgets to effect control works not only on the executive level, but right down to the department as well. In one company, budgets were prepared and controlled on the departmental level. Accounting analyzed each account monthly and compared it to budget, and in some cases prepared a simple chart to show trends.

During the first six months of the year, actual office supply expenses began exceeding budget by a growing margin, as shown in Figure 2-1. The manager had been keeping an eye on this account, but was not concerned until June, when the negative trend appeared to be established beyond a doubt.

Figure 2–1

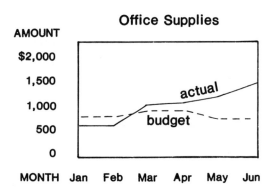

expense analysis

Upon analysis, the following was discovered:

1. The department increased its employees from 11 to 19. This meant additional supply costs, which were not budgeted.
2. This year's budget was projected to be similar to the previous year's. However, two major suppliers had instituted price increases averaging 5%.
3. In the previous year a supplier had offered a 4% discount for payment of bills by the tenth of the month, but that policy was not in effect this year.

These three factors were seen as causes of the unfavorable variance. The fault was both in assumptions and unknown changes in conditions. But actual supply expenses were not unreasonable, considering all the factors. The manager's recommendation read:

> The current budget for office supplies should be modified to reflect existing conditions:
>
> 1. A 73% increase in staff in the department, not anticipated in the original budget.
> 2. Price increases by suppliers.
> 3. Loss of discounts allowed in the past by one major supplier.

The alternative would be to live with the unfavorable variances, or to suggest an increase in the budget without revealing underlying causes. In a situation where actual expenses run ahead of budgets, it is natural to assume the problem is in control. One possible response might be to put into effect rigid systems for centralized responsibility, requisitioning, or other measures, but while these ideas are appropriate in some circumstances, they do not apply here. Controls might curtail personal usage and make employees aware of budgetary restraints. But in the end, the real problem—that the budget was inadequate for the level of expense—would be unaddressed.

It is proper to take action in response to discovered trends. And in the example above, the department actually made that trend visible by placing it on a chart. Once the problem is known, the next step is to identify causes. Arbitrary budget assumptions provide no basis upon which to discover causes. For example, an office supply budget may be written to run 10%

higher than the average levels of the previous year. Using that procedure gives no way to identify the causes of a variance. But understanding the contributing factors—new employees, higher prices, elimination of discounts—makes the cause of the variance clear.

The office supplies account provides a good example of the control problem every manager faces, because it seems to create problems in every company. Whether the cause is pilferage, poor budgeting, growth in the number of employees, or changing prices, the real difficulty is in knowing how to defend the budget, react to variances, or decide upon controls.

In one company, an executive complained about variances in office supplies by saying, "How many pencils can our employees go through in one month?" Without a strong and detailed assumption base in the budget, there's no easy answer to that question. Factors to keep in mind:

1. If the number of employees increases, so will office supply costs. And a massive expansion of markets will also require a larger support staff . . . thus, more money for office supplies.
2. "Supplies" are more than pencils and other small-cost items. Examining what goes into the account often shows that it is used as a catch-all for miscellaneous expenses and is subject to widespread abuse. For example, equipment maintenance and leasing costs, printing, and other expenses that warrant their own accounts may all be lumped into "supplies."
3. Price increases will add to supply costs significantly. Analyze two previous years' invoices to get a sense of cost trends. The wide range of different types of items makes this difficult, so perform your analysis on the basis of costs for commonly purchased items, selecting a few that recur monthly.

The analytical approach can be applied to any account, and most will not be as complicated as office supplies. The more detailed your research is, the better your assumption will be. And assumptions based on specifics provide a way to identify flaws when variances do occur.

The goal of budgeting should not be to entirely eliminate its inevitable flaws. In that respect, nobody can expect the budget to predict the future accurately. The real intention in budgeting is to build procedures for making distinctions. Are your assumptions wrong? If so, the budget should be changed at once. Or, do you have a control problem in the current level of spending? If so, you will then know what actions must be taken to bring the expense into line.

The same argument applies to forecasting income. If actual income falls behind the forecast, why? Was the forecast too aggressive, too unrealistic? Were key factors left out, such as an allowance for attrition among the existing sales force? If so, the assumption must be changed. But if the assumption is realistic, then the corrective action is to suggest monthly volume goals on the regional and individual levels.

WORK PROJECT

1. Printing expenses in your department are running 18% above budget. Identify three possible causes of the problem.

2. Income for the first quarter is far below the forecast level. The assumption was made that the estimated 714 salespeople would average $9,500 in volume per month. You discover that the sales force now includes 723 people, but they are averaging only $7,250 each. What suggestions would you make?

3. You want to hire an additional employee because workloads are much greater than anyone thought last year. But the budget does not include new hires. What arguments could you make to support your request?

3

The Secret of Income Forecasting

Prophecy is the most gratuitous form of error.

—George Eliot

An income forecast for the new year was prepared by the accounting department of a real estate management company, consisting of one figure for each month, but without further explanation. When the president asked how the numbers had been developed he was told, "We know we're going to spend at least that much, because the expense budgets have already been done. But we did add a factor to allow for a modest profit."

This "backwards budgeting" is the most popular method for forecasting income. Unfortunately, several flaws mar this approach. First, it is a passive method that does not examine the potential for growth in income (or spot trouble in the near future). Second, it gives no means for explaining variances throughout the year. And third, preparation of income forecasts must precede expense budgeting.

24

THE FORECAST AS A PRIORITY

It makes sense to forecast income as a first step in the overall budgeting process. So many variable expenses will change based on the assumptions that go into income that it simply isn't practical to do it any other way.

The income forecast is a financial expression of the policies management sets for the new year. So as a first rule of effective forecasting, management must dictate the criteria for developing numbers. This is not to say that the president of the company must sit down and work out the monthly income levels. But goals for marketing, investment, and pricing must all be explained in specific terms by management before budgets are prepared.

For example, the accountant of an insurance agency was instructed to prepare the annual budget, but without information from the president about expectations for the new year. As a result, income forecasts were based on average volume for the previous year. Upon review, the president revealed his intention to expand operations and increase gross income by 30%. This was not reflected in the forecast. The new information meant revising the forecast and several related expenses. To increase revenue forecasts, it was also necessary to increase assumptions about the level of certain variable expenses:

Commissions—based directly on sales, this account had to be increased 30% along with sales.

Salaries and wages—the requirement necessitated a larger support staff.

Travel and entertainment—more income means more clients, more sales reps, and more out-of-town meetings.

Telephone—more calls out of town.

Other expenses—office supplies, printing, postage, and payroll taxes were all estimated to run at higher levels because of increased income.

Problems can arise when income forecasts are changed after expense budgets are estimated. In one publishing company an annual forecast and budget was submitted to the executive vice president for review. He approved the expense budgets but increased income forecasts. He provided no written justification for the change, making it the most difficult form of change to live with. Not only did his action make meaningful variance explanations impossible, it also threw off the direct ratio between income and expenses.

There is no easy solution to this problem, especially when you are responsible for explaining why something went wrong, but with numbers manipulated beyond your control. Minimize this problem, however, by basing everything on solid assumptions. Then if management makes changes it is more likely to refer to the assumption base along with the final numbers.

You can put this approach into practice with relative ease and still relate with discretion to your supervisor or even the company president. It is not prudent to respond to an arbitrary change by saying, "You can't do that. There's no logical reason." Instead, refer back to your assumptions and ask which part of them is being changed.

For example, the executive vice president of a management consultation firm reviewed the forecast for the coming year that had been prepared by the firm's accountant. It was broken down into several types of income, both for existing contracts and projected new clients. When the vice president wanted to increase the forecast by $6,000 per month, the accountant asked, "Are we changing the forecast for our existing accounts, or for new ones?" The vice president responded that estimates of new account revenues should be higher. So the accountant documented the adjustment by noting the source for the change, and commented that certain general expenses would have to be reviewed as well.

By following this procedure, arbitrary changes are noted or, more appropriately, executives desiring to make such changes are forced to identify which assumption they are questioning. Then, if unfavorable variances do occur later, the causes can be identified precisely.

DEVELOPING A STRONG ASSUMPTION BASE

Every organization has a logical and specific means for building an assumption base. Some form of "units of production" can be applied logically even in the most difficult of circumstances.

For example, the owner of an employment agency insisted that there was no way to project future revenues. The characteristics of this business did, in fact, make that task especially elusive. Little if any repeat business occurred, and income depended on the state of the job market. How could future income be predicted accurately?

In cases like this, the assumption base should start with an analysis of the past. Of course, future income cannot be derived entirely from past trends, but some factors will affect the income forecast, such as:

1. seasonal trends
2. minimum and maximum monthly income
3. market conditions

For the employment agency, the seasonal trend turned out to be fairly predictable. The best months for business were June and July, and the worst months were November and December. The analysis of this trend showed that a natural cresting in the summer months had occurred every year for the past four years, as shown in Figure 3-1.

Figure 3–1

seasonal trends

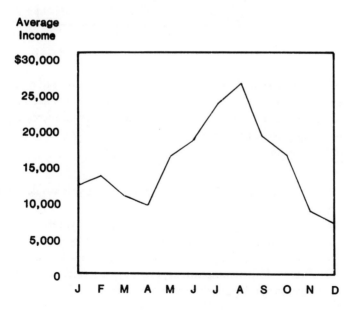

The second part of the analysis—minimum and maximum income—
was also analyzed over the four years the agency had been in business. Not
only was the monthly base increased each year; the gap in the range was
growing as well, as shown in Figure 3-2.

Figure 3–2

minimum/maximum income

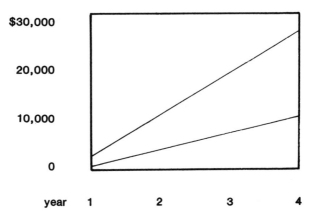

The third test, that of market conditions, was an analysis of recent employment trends. The owner saw that volume of placements had been low
two years before, but the previous year's numbers showed increasing employment trends in the area. This led to the development of some assumptions for the coming year:

1. That the volume of placements in the coming year would increase
   by 5%.
2. That the seasonal pattern established in the past would continue.
3. That minimum monthly income would grow by $1,000 over the
   previous year and that maximum potential revenues would increase
   by $3,000. This assumption kept income forecasts in realistic per-
   spective, given the growth pattern in the past.

In the process of developing assumptions, the owner also noted that of the five employment agencies in the area one year before, two had gone out of business. This further supported the contention that income could be expected to increase in the coming year.

Depending on the nature of services or products a company markets, the logical assumption base may be much more tangible. For example, in any business that depends on direct sales, forecasts should be based on average production, especially when salespeople are paid by commissions.

A securities broker-dealer prepared its forecast in detail, with the assumption resting on recruitment and average production figures. An analysis of the previous year revealed the following facts:

1. The average representative with the firm for three years or more produced gross income averaging $16,300 per month. A commission of 60% was paid to the representative, with 40% retained by the broker-dealer. A three-year analysis also revealed that the average monthly gross had increased each year by 8%.
2. Representatives with the firm for more than one year but less than three years averaged $11,800 per month.
3. Representatives with less than one year's experience averaged $5,800 per month. In the average case, production was not booked until the representative had been working for three months.
4. Attrition rates for the three categories were also analyzed. The following termination rates were discovered:

3 + years	1–3 years	0–1 year
4%	16%	42%

The income forecast was prepared based on these facts and figures. An additional assumption was made that the firm would recruit at least 11 new representatives per month, adding to its existing sales force of 210.

Now the assumption can be prepared with a thorough breakdown. Recruitment assumptions, historical production separated by years of experience and modified by attrition, and a modest assumption about increases in average production all add up to a solid income forecast. And during the year, variances can be tied directly to recruitment, true averages, and attrition—dependable and recognizable attributes for this type of firm.

Some organizations have a similar assumption base but a less specific method for predicting volume. For example, one book publisher estimates its revenues based on three factors:

1. Continuing sales of books on its existing list,
2. Estimates of revenues for soon-to-be-released books,
3. Revenues from subsidiary rights (book clubs, paperback and foreign rights, and licensing fees for video and audio cassettes).

All of these must be estimated, using reasonable historical information and in consideration of the market. The forecast must also depend on the nature of books being released and demand for those books, the type of market, and ways of reaching it. Competition is also a significant factor. Book publishers and other businesses heavily dependent on estimates must use historical information and modify their estimates for market considerations more than those with direct salespeople, where income is more connected to recruitment and direct marketing management.

A third type of income forecasting, centered on the client base, is most appropriate in strictly service organizations. For example, one professional corporation forecasts its revenues based on known and existing contracts and estimates of its ability to attract new clients during the coming year. Another attribute of this type of company is the limitation of people versus time. When the product is billed by the hour, income is limited and specifiable. Professional services (like law and accounting firms, physicians, engineers, architects, and consultants) must forecast income based on these limitations. A law firm cannot count on 40 hours a week of billable time for every attorney on staff, because some time must be spent on administrative details, meetings, and transportation. Thus forecasts must consider the ratio of billable hours as a limitation of potential income.

TESTING ASSUMPTIONS

Despite the importance of developing a logical and sound assumption base, it will not necessarily be the only way to prepare the forecast. Two or more alternatives are usually available. What then is the test for reliability?

One consulting firm faced this issue when two versions of an income forecast were prepared—one by the senior marketing vice president and another by the chief accountant. The marketing point of view was to assume a specific number of new clients during the year (with that forecast also recommending retaining additional professional staffing). The accountant's forecast was based on an analysis of billable hours and existing contracts. The final results were several thousands of dollars apart.

Both forecasts had merit. While it's unusual for two people to be preparing the same forecast at the same time, you might experience a similar conflict in trying to select the better method to justify your forecast. The solution: Work out both methods and then look for a compromise. In the case of the consulting firm, the limitations expressed in the accounting version (in terms of billable hours and recent trends) were used to modify the marketing version. A somewhat less optimistic forecast was settled upon, recognizing that growth in permanent clients would probably proceed at a slower rate than marketing had predicted; and that hiring new professional staff members should be done on a more cautious schedule than originally planned.

Assumptions should be tested against historical fact. In one situation, a company's revenues were derived from the efforts of a sales force. The original forecast calculated new recruits but contained two flaws: First, income was estimated to be booked in the same month that new salespeople joined the firm, where history showed there was a 90- to 120-day delay. Second, no allowance was made for terminations. Again, history proved that no fewer than one-third of new commission-based salespeople were gone within the first year. So the original forecast was adjusted to more closely estimate what was likely to occur. When estimating income, always look for offsets to the original forecast. Every example of growth contains minor setbacks along the way. Whether it's an aggressive recruitment drive (with some attrition) or the introduction of new products (with some percentage of them failing), allow for contingencies. A forecast that assumes a perfect year will be flawed.

CONTROL OF GROWTH LEVELS

Flawed income assumptions have ramifications far beyond unfavorable variances on the top line. Management decisions based on an overly optimistic growth curve can lead to severe losses and a disruption of operations throughout the year.

For example, a software consultation and development firm estimated growth both in existing contracts and in new client contracts for the coming year. Income was forecast to increase more than 70%. This led to adjustments in the expense budget and plans to increase the staff from 14 to 22. That also meant a demand for larger facilities. By the end of the first quarter, the company relocated to an office with twice as much space, and hired eight additional staff members.

By the end of the third quarter, two major accounts were gone. One went out of business and the other changed systems, eliminating the need for continuing help. In addition, the projected growth in new clients had been overly optimistic. It appeared that income for the entire year would rise by less than 15%, rather than the estimated 70% in the forecast.

The company was now committed to a lease that cost twice as much as the previous one, and had to lay off six of the eight new employees. They were showing a net loss for the year and expected severe cash flow problems for at least the next six months.

In this example, a forecast of higher revenues inspired management to increase overhead. If the forecast had been accurate, those higher levels would have been justified. But no room was left for the inevitable contingencies. A more cautious schedule would have deferred moving until later, and would have called for hiring new people only after the demand occurred.

Increased income rarely occurs in a straight line, even though most forecasts project it that way. To achieve a realistic forecast, allow for the temporary setbacks to be expected in any company. Quality permanent growth takes time, and realistic forecasting depends on making allowances, anticipating setbacks, and cautiously planning increased overhead only *after* considering what could go wrong. While income forecasts are only estimates, commitments like salaries and wages to new employees or long-term leases on new facilities tend to be permanent.

Including contingencies in the forecast but still assuming growth uses the process to increase performance. For example, in one direct marketing company, the marketing director developed a forecast that was broken down by individual sales offices. He used the forecast as an annual goal for each office, and budgeted incentives for managers to meet or surpass their goal. As a result, the year's income exceeded the forecast.

In that case, the forecast was more than an attempt to anticipate future trends in sales volume. It became a marketing tool to set goals for offices and even individual salespeople. Good forecasts can apply this way in many cases—especially when volume success is directly tied to individual productivity. The exercise then becomes a source for profitable volume, and goes far beyond the administrative necessity of responsible forecasting.

WORK PROJECT

1. A software development company recently introduced two new products to the market. It's too soon to tell how well these products are selling. What criteria would you use to forecast the year's income?

2. Your marketing department has enthusiastically forecast a 100% growth in sales volume because of its aggressive campaign to recruit new sales representatives. What cautionary adjustments would you recommend in modifying this forecast?

3. Based on estimates of substantial growth, the company may need to hire several new employees, install a phone system with greater capacity, and move to larger quarters—all within the next year. How do you suggest proceeding within this forecast to avoid problems of excessive overhead? What factors should be considered in a revised forecast?

4

Building Your Expense Budget Base

When eating an elephant, take one bite at a time.

—General Creighton Abrams

"Why is it that every time I submit a budget, it gets cut?" one manager complained. His friend, a more experienced manager with the same company, answered, "Because you don't make a good case for yourself. If you line up your expenses like ducks, they're easy to shoot down. The answer is to make them look like eagles."

It's not enough to just submit numbers. To get a budget approved, you must be able to back up what you turn in. A successful budget is based not just on accurate numbers or reasonable estimates. It must also be accompanied by proof. That proof sells your ideas and means developing sound assumptions and communicating them to your supervisor or to other budget reviewers.

BUILDING ASSUMPTIONS

Building strong and supportable assumptions uses the same procedure, whatever the type of budget.

34

For example, the marketing department of a company found a way to use budgeting to sell a proposal for an expanded commission and sales reporting system. The system involved development of a new format for monthly commission statements, breakdowns of sales in greater detail, and improved status checks from remote terminals. The marketing manager's proposal included a budget estimating the cost of development. He consulted with the data processing department to estimate the time involved, and built a specific series of assumptions.

That wasn't enough. The estimate itself could be cut—or even turned down entirely. So the manager expanded the proposal by adding two elements. First was an explanation of how assumptions had been derived. Second was an explanation of how the company would benefit by investing in the expanded system. His report:

Proposal: Expanded Marketing System

The marketing department proposes the development of an improved reporting system for sales and commissions. We contend that a decision to approve this report will result in greater efficiency and increased volume and profits, and that the cost of this project will be recaptured in less than one year.

This proposal will require a commitment of 120 hours of EDP staff time over the next three months as well as the purchase of 11 new remote terminals.

Background: During the four years our present system has been in use, the sales force has grown by 318%. Total sales volume during this period has increased by more than 500%. The present system, however, does not provide the following:

1. the ability for sales managers or individual salespeople to review their status during the month;
2. breakdowns of sales by region or individual; or
3. division of commissions by product.

Assumptions: The marketing department has prepared a detailed description of the system it needs for its sales force, including sample reporting forms and a description of remote access capabilities. This summary has been reviewed by the manager of our EDP department, and a cost estimate has been prepared. A summary:

1. EDP staff time: 120 hours, at $17 per hour (average), total $2,040.
2. Outside consultation for the development of additional programming: 15 hours, at $85 per hour, total $1,275.
3. Purchase of 11 access terminals, $1,150 each, total $12,650.

(Note: a detailed breakdown of costs is attached.)

This project can be completed within three months from approval date. The marketing and EDP departments have agreed upon a tentative completion schedule.

Benefits: The company will benefit directly from installation of a more convenient sales reporting system. For a total cost of less than $16,000, the improved reporting will enable sales managers to motivate individual salespeople and to better manage quotas.

Training and support are not budgeted as a separate item, but are considered part of the ongoing service provided by the EDP department. The cost of new terminals includes initial orientation and support from the manufacturer.

The company has emphasized the importance of motivating individual salespeople to establish and meet goals for volume of business, and management has suggested the development of a competitive spirit between regions. In addition, sales incentives programs have been recommended as part of this program. The installation of this system will enable sales personnel to regularly review their progress and to implement management's suggestions.

In addition to the motivational advantages this system will offer, an upgraded reporting capability will better serve the purposes of regional sales managers, through immediate review and reporting capability. A common complaint the marketing department hears is that statistics are not available for a given month until the middle of the following month. This new system will enable those managers to review progress weekly, even daily if desired. Each of the 11 regional managers will be able to track progress as frequently as necessary, thus spotting and correcting negative volume trends as they occur, and not many weeks after.

We conservatively estimate that this improved system will increase average sales volume by 4%. However, even an improvement of half that level will justify a decision to go ahead.

With only a 2% increase in average sales volume, this new system will pay for itself in less than nine months. (Average monthly volume for the last six months = $1.3 million. Average net profit of 7% = $91,000. A 2% increase will equal $1,820 per month.)

This proposal is based on research, especially with the manager of the department that will have to do the work. It contains several key elements that make a proposal successful, notably a well-supported budget. This is summarized in Figure 4-1.

Figure 4–1

elements of the proposal

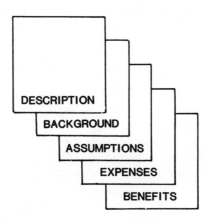

Follow the outlined steps included in "Elements of Successful Proposals" in developing your own proposals.

For specific projects, a detailed report that follows this outline enables management to make a decision based on the merits of your proposal. Are your assumptions sound? Are they realistic? The building of absolutely solid

---

Elements of Successful Proposals

1. Description. What is your proposal? Explain exactly what you're asking for.
2. Background. Describe the current environment and include relevant statistics. If you are asking for an upgrade, tell how long the current system has been in effect and compare that to growth.
3. Assumptions. Explain how you developed your proposal. Did you speak with other managers, outside vendors, or specialists? Explain your assumptions for cost, time, and efficiency.
4. Expense. Present your budget in summary and attach detailed expense information as a separate section of the proposal. If the project is especially complex, include a timetable that breaks it down into specific progress steps.
5. Benefits. You're asking the company to give you a budget. How will this expenditure benefit in the long run? Rather than simply asking for a sum of money, show how your idea will either increase profits directly, cut other expenses, or improve service.

---

assumptions is at the root of successful budgeting, whether for a special project or for a departmental or companywide budget.

TAILORING ASSUMPTIONS

Every expense you budget should be fully supported with the proper and most logical assumption you can develop. Avoid simply estimating, which is the least supportable form of budgeting.

Finding the logical assumption depends on an examination of the components of an expense. In the example above, the project had three parts: internal commitment of time, which would cost the company money through the payroll system; consulting expenses; and an investment in terminals for each branch office. For some types of projects or expenses, assumptions are very obvious; for others, analysis or research will be required.

Four primary elements are in every assumption:

1. Information sources. The components of each expense category will dictate the source for information. Rent is contained in a contract that will dictate exactly what the company will spend in the

contracted period. More complicated and variable expenses like entertainment will depend on the number of people authorized to spend money, historical levels of expenditure, and estimates of future sales.

2. Growth. If the income forecast predicts substantial growth, budget variable expenses accordingly. A variable is any expense likely to change with the volume of sales (travel and entertainment, telephone, and advertising, for example).

3. Timing. After identifying the causes of an expense level, decide when the expense will occur. In an advertising budget, the logical timing assumption will be related directly to campaigns and to an understanding of seasonal markets. If the budget plan calls for a staff expansion, expenses such as office supplies and telephone can be modified along the same time line.

4. Controls. An assumption must take into account controls that are either already in place or proposed. For example, if the current year's telephone expenses seem unreasonably high, use a telephone log to prevent unauthorized use. Or if pilferage of office supplies is suspected, the company may centralize control and install a requisitioning system.

The four elements of the assumption are summarized in Figure 4-2.

Figure 4-2

elements of the assumption

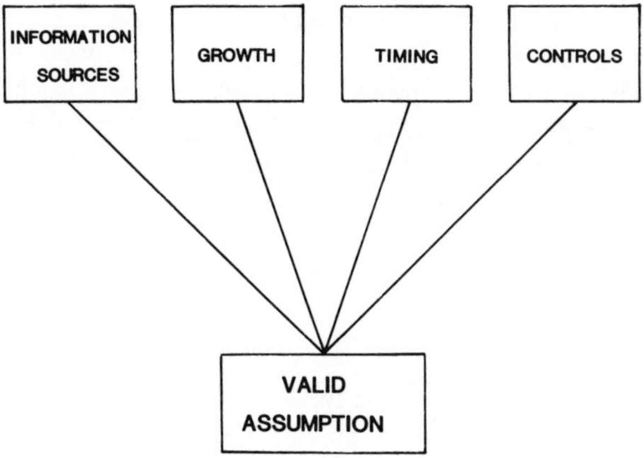

Applying these four elements will make your expense assumptions valid and lead to a better acceptance ratio of your budget proposals by management. For some expenses (like rent), where the level is usually known in advance, the process is simple. But consider all four elements for every expense, even those for which budgeting appears simple. For example, for rent:

Information source: The rental contract.

Growth: If your company plans a large expansion, will that include many more employees? If so, are present facilities adequate to house them? A move during the year would directly affect a rent budget.

Timing: Is the present contract scheduled to expire this year? If so, do you have a renewal option? Renewals are usually accompanied by a higher monthly fee.

Controls: Usually not applicable.

For some expense categories, the four elements involve more complex possibilities. Two accounts—office supplies and travel and entertainment—present the greatest budgeting problems in most organizations for several reasons:

1. Many companies allow these expenses to accumulate passively. There are no preapproval controls in place. Thus, any number of employees can contribute to a budget variance.

2. Variances may be caused by coding problems. Many expenses are coded to office supplies rather than other accounts (such as printing, equipment leasing, postage, promotion), or to travel and entertainment (such as convention and meeting expenses or advertising). This makes accurate budgeting more difficult.

3. Controls are often unenforced or nonexistent.

4. Abuse of budget levels often occurs at the top levels in the company, making enforcement of the budget impracticable.

So how can you effectively budget for and control these problem accounts? Following is a review of how to apply the four assumption elements:

Office Supplies:

> *Information sources:* Check invoices and statements from suppliers you use regularly. Look for a trend in pricing. How often are prices increased, and how much? Consider the benefits of volume purchasing, discounts allowed for prompt payment, and pricing by the competition. Many of the large-volume items frequently purchased may be available at discount through catalog purchasing.

> *Growth:* Is the company increasing the number of employees? If the current budget calls for new hires, include an increase in office supply expenses on an expense-per-employee basis. Office supply expenses can and should be analyzed and estimated on this basis.

> *Timing:* If you purchase a large volume of supplies to take advantage of discounts, when will those purchases occur? Obviously, if you follow this strategy, your supply expenses will not be even throughout the year. If new employees are scheduled, increase per-employee expenses according to the time of hire. Where several factors are used for the assumption, detail them on a worksheet, as shown in Figure 4-3.

> *Controls:* A centralized supply purchasing system in a large company may involve establishing a separate department to buy, store, distribute, and control. In a smaller setting, departmental controls may be effective. Other controls might include a requisition approval system, lock-up of supplies, or storage in view of a supervisor or several employees. Since controls are usually intended to discourage and prevent pilferage, taking appropriate steps may effect a significant drop in expenses.

Travel and entertainment T+E:

> *Information sources:* Depend on the historical record to develop the initial base. In companies where individuals project their own T+E expenses, the budgeting process involves review and consolidation upon approval of estimates. This is often the case when many marketing and sales employees are on the payroll.

> *Growth:* This is a strictly variable expense. The level of T+E will depend on executive and sales activity. So when a substantial increase in the volume of sales is projected, travel and entertainment must be increased accordingly.

Figure 4-3

timing worksheet

Expense _____ Year _____

MONTH	1	2	3	4	5
Jan					
Feb					
Mar					
Apr					
May					
Jun					
Jul					
Aug					
Sep					
Oct					
Nov					
Dec					

EXPLANATION

1 _____

2 _____

3 _____

4 _____

5 _____

Timing: Budget this expense keeping in mind seasonal volume. An analysis of past sales volume and travel and entertainment might provide guidelines for estimating future levels in this category.

Controls: Companies may strictly limit the authorization for T+E among the sales staff and executives. A review and approval procedure should include reimbursement based on submission of an expense report with receipts attached. Also suggest using a responsible travel agency that will get the best discount fares for executive travel and acceptable economy rates and corporate discounts from hotels.

TESTING ASSUMPTIONS

Even the most complete assumption may be challenged in review. Either build an extra allowance into the budget (assuming it will be cut), or challenge and modify the assumptions yourself before submitting them.

Taking the first approach is a negative form of budgeting. Adding fat to a budget is a violation of the basic premise that the numbers you develop are, in fact, your best estimates.

Look for flaws in your assumptions. Before submitting the budget, try to perfect all of the elements in each assumption, proving that you have looked for every conceivable way to (a) eliminate unnecessary expenses, (b) develop money-saving control ideas, and (c) anticipate levels of expense that might otherwise be overlooked.

For example, you have prepared a budget for telephone expense for the coming year. Part of your assumption is that expenses will increase in line with expected staff increases. That appears logical at first. But will those employees be using the phone? And if so, will their calls be made on the same basis as that of the "average" employee? A large portion of the company's phone expenses may involve long-distance calls made by executives and salespeople. If the new employees will be clerical, applying an average increase based strictly on a per-employee usage factor may be unreasonable.

A second element of your telephone expense budget assumes that last year's expense level will be continued to the following year. But what would be the effect of installing new controls such as a phone log and an announcement that personal calls may not be made on company phones? Simply making this statement often will eliminate many examples of abuse and could result in lower expense.

A third element may be related to the type of growth levels predicted. For example your company plans to open offices 2,000 miles away. That means a higher volume of long-distance calls. Or plans call for the installation of a toll-free customer service line—again, a higher expense that you might overlook.

Test your assumptions critically, examining them from every possible angle. If the company expects you to develop a budget for variable expenses, insist on being allowed to review income forecasts and any marketing plans. If your budget will be affected by decisions made on the executive and marketing levels, you should know about them and incorporate these estimates into your budget.

Review assumptions remembering these factors:

1. Income forecasts,
2. Market expansion plans,
3. Number of employees planned,
4. Possible price increases,
5. Elimination of markets, product lines, or other forms of consolidation,
6. Administrative changes, such as centralization of supply or printing costs, changes in telephone systems, or additions of new services or departments.

Be prepared to answer any questions about your assumptions, remembering that the more thorough your preparatory research, the less likely your budgets will be changed. The successful budget proposal (meaning the one in which the fewest changes are made and the fewest variances occur) is the one that is well documented and supported with facts.

THE INFLATION FACTOR

The most common budget development method is assuming a general rise in prices. This is a flawed budgeting procedure, because it fails to credit the effects or even the potential of controls. It also fails to adjust for other changes, such as expanded markets and services, an increase in the employee population, or forecasts of higher—or lower—gross income.

The inflation factor also makes it impossible to intelligently explain a variance when it does occur. Explanations like the following are seen in many reports:

> The budget assumed that average expenses would increase by 3% for the year. To date, actual expenses exceed last year's levels by nearly 5%.

What does this tell management? What measures should be taken to reverse the unfavorable variance? Or should a flaw in the assumption be recognized and corrected? This variance explanation gives nothing of value to the reviewer because the initial assumption itself is of no value.

A flaw that often shows up under this method is the belief that inflation is to blame. If you budget an expense at "3% above last year's level" and you then experience a variance, what is the real cause?

If prices are truly higher than you expected, you should be able to prove that with facts and figures:

> Office supply variances are caused by unanticipated price increases by suppliers. We budgeted a 5% increase, but average prices rose by more than 7%.

It is more often the case that prices have not risen significantly—but spending levels have. That would indicate a serious control problem, one that demands action. A negative trend can be controlled only if it is identified and corrective action indicated. An assumption based on a percentage increase cannot show whether a variance is due to price increases or, more likely, that spending levels are too high.

One way to ensure the validity of the assumptions in your budget is to be aware of problems that could occur during the year. If you would have difficulty explaining a variance, examine your assumptions one more time. Find any flaws in what you have prepared, and put in a little more work to perfect your estimate. By following this standard, and by applying the four elements of assumptions to every account, you will become an effective budget manager.

WORK PROJECT

1. Your office supplies account has always presented a problem, usually reporting unfavorable variances. You identify the problem as a combination of coding and lack of control systems. What steps should you take in developing your assumptions, and what recommendations for change might you suggest?

2. List four sources for information needed to estimate next year's budget for travel and entertainment, and to build a valid assumption base.

3. You submit a proposal for the installation of a new terminal in your department, to improve access to a centralized system. Your supervisor responds by telling you it's too expensive and will have to wait. In resubmitting your idea, what sources can you use to show support for your contention that the company will profit from approving your idea?

5

Staying in the Black

A man who has a million dollars is as well off as if he were rich.

—John Jacob Astor III

Two managers were discussing their personal finances at lunch. One, named Sue, complained that even with a higher income this year than last, she always seemed to be in debt and out of cash. The other asked her how much income would be enough. Sue thought about it a moment and answered, "I don't just need income. I need disposable income."

We all tend to increase our standard of living to match or slightly surpass our income. To an individual, careful money management means planning, even if only on a monthly basis. Ironically, while we as individuals are concerned with the availability of cash, we often overlook this need in business. The emphasis is usually on profits. And it is possible to show a decent profit and still be "cash poor," a problem that can lead to business failure or the inability to take advantage of market opportunities.

One company, for example, had experienced cash flow problems for the past two years, due to a growing level of outstanding accounts receivable, a high level of debt, and the purchase of capital assets without a coordinated plan. When a competitor went out of business, the investment capital simply wasn't available and the company couldn't take over new territories. The company lost the opportunity to its competitors.

WORKING CAPITAL CONTROLS

The process of creating responsible cash management controls is mysterious to many executives and managers, partially because of the emphasis on the "bottom line." In the effort to earn an acceptable level of profit, not enough thought goes into the importance of maintaining working capital.

Monitoring the relationship between current assets (cash, accounts receivable, inventory, and other assets that are convertible to cash within 12 months) and current liabilities (debts payable within 12 months) is one method for spotting cash flow trends. The difference between these groupings of accounts is referred to as working capital:

$$\begin{array}{r} \text{Current assests} \\ - \ \underline{\text{Current liabilities}} \\ \text{Working capital} \end{array}$$

As a general rule, the ratio should be maintained at 2 to 1 or better. For example, if current liabilities are $245,000, current assets should be $490,000 or higher. In companies that do not maintain inventories of tangible products, this ratio does not apply. Instead, the quick assets ratio is used. It's the same formula (current assets divided by current liabilities). But the minimum acceptable level should be 1 to 1 or better. The three working capital tests are summarized in Figure 5-1.

Trends in working capital in many companies are affected by seasonal volume. While overhead expenses remain constant (meaning a constant drain on available cash), income levels may drop, which results in a deterioration in working capital. In those situations, a seasonal dip is inevitable. To survive requires planning for several months in advance.

For example, an office development and design firm gained most of its contracts during the spring and summer months, but business was virtually dead in the winter. Maintaining an office year-round made it necessary to control cash throughout the year. Usually during five months expenses exceeded income. That meant setting aside reserves when cash was available and using the excess during the lean months. The technique requires discipline and careful budgeting, but is necessary to get through the year. When all factors—income, expenses, and payments on account—are exactly the same throughout the year, cash control is simple, but that rarely occurs.

Figure 5–1

working capital tests

WORKING CAPITAL

current assets
− current liabilities

CURRENT RATIO

$$\frac{\text{current assets}}{\text{current liabilities}}$$

QUICK ASSETS RATIO

$$\frac{\text{current assets without inventory}}{\text{current liabilities}}$$

This seasonal swing is experienced in several industries. The problem is summarized in Figure 5-2. A company may be profitable for the year as a whole and still have deficits for nearly half the year. In some small retail businesses, cash is drained for nine or ten months, and made up during the

Christmas season—an extreme case, to be sure, but one that demonstrates the amount of forward thinking necessary to stay in business.

Figure 5–2

the seasonal factor

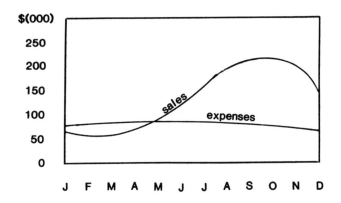

Those who do not plan in advance must go into debt every year, hoping to come out ahead during a profitable season. It doesn't take much to push the situation far enough that debt eventually overtakes income. In this way many poorly financed businesses end up closing their doors. The problem often exists in larger companies as well, to varying degrees, but it can often be eliminated or modified with good advance planning.

What can you do to reverse a negative trend in cash flow? Some analysts passively accept the problem, believing they can take no immediate steps to offset such a trend. But in fact there are many moves you can either take yourself or suggest to management. As part of a manager's job, anticipating the future through the recognition of trends should be a natural function. And recommending action or policies involves projection control (see "Working Capital Controls").

Working Capital Controls

Cash:
- Create and fund reserves for anticipated slow months.
- Invest temporarily available funds in interest-bearing but liquid accounts.
- Suggest advance planning for the purchase of capital assets. Sell obsolete or unneeded assets.

Accounts receivable:
- Tighten up collection procedures on existing accounts.
- Improve procedures for granting credit to new customers or clients.
- Introduce discounts for prompt payment and late charges for past-due accounts.

Inventory:
- Avoid excessive volume purchases.
- Control stock with revolving partial counts, concentrating on problem areas.
- Lock up inventory subject to high levels of pilferage, and count frequently.

Debts:
- Enforce internal controls over levels of purchasing for office supplies, printing, and other overhead accounts.
- Cut back on expense commitment levels when purchasing activity has been excessive; review existing controls and suggest improvements.
- Avoid new loan commitments and consider negotiating a revised repayment schedule for existing debt.

DEVELOPING THE ASSUMPTION

Watching and controlling working capital trends is a necessary and important management task. But equally crucial is the development of a cash flow projection, as part of the budgeting process.

Management tends to concentrate on income and expenses and to ignore cash flow except in a backward-looking review—a sign of the common preoccupation with profits. Even with a large surplus of cash available, ignoring cash flow does cost money—through a failure to control collections, inventory, and the acquisition or disposal of capital assets.

For most companies, cash flow projections should be included in the budgeting process. This requires the development of a month-to-month projection set up on the same format as an income forecast or expense budget. It is not enough to prepare a Sources and Applications of Funds Statement (one of three forms of financial statements, the other two being the balance sheet and the income statement). This report is useful, but it does not provide the means for control; it only reports on what has occurred in the past (see "The Third Financial Statement").

The sources and applications of funds statement is a status report that shows what's occurred in the past. Just as an income statement cannot be thought of as a means for control of expense levels, the sources and applications of funds statement does nothing to help control the future availability of working capital.

The Third Financial Statement

Balance sheets and income statements are familiar, but a third type of financial statement is not well understood. That's the Sources and Applications of Funds Statement (also called Cash Flow Statement or Summary of Cash Flow). An example is shown in Figure 5-3.

This statement contains two major parts:

Part I

This is a summary of sources and applications, including net profits (adjusted for noncash expenses), increases in long-term liabilities (such as loan proceeds) decreases in long-term asset accounts, and cash received from the sale of capital assets. Following these items is a summary of applications, such as cash used to purchase capital assets, and decreases in long-term liabilities (like repayments on loans). The difference between the increases and decreases is the change for the year in working capital.

Part II

This shows which current asset and liability accounts make up the change. The net increase or decrease in current accounts balances with the Part I breakdown.

Figure 5-3

Sources and Applications of Funds Statement

January 1 to December 31, 19 –

PART I

Sources of Funds:

Net profits	$147,613
Less: non-cash expenses	(18,550)
Increase in long-term liabilities	13,046
Sale of capital assets	15,000
Proceeds of loans	35,000
Total sources of funds	$192,109

Applications of Funds:

Purchase of capital assets	$ 98,000
Payments on loans	16,460
Investment in subsidiary	47,948
Total applications of funds	$162,408
Increase in Working Capital	$ 29,701

PART II

Cash	$13,011
Accounts receivable	(2,491)
Notes receivable	16,000
Accounts payable	14,502
Current notes payable	(11,321)
Increase	$29,701

To control the future, a "sources and aps" statement must be prepared in advance, based on sound assumptions and research. Consider the impact on cash flow of all relevant factors that you now know:

1. Forecast income, expenses, and net profits
2. Adjustments for noncash expenses, such as depreciation
3. Current loans outstanding
4. Anticipated collections of accounts receivable
5. Estimated payment of accounts and taxes payable

Also consider the possible changes during the coming year:

1. New loan commitments
2. Acquisitions of capital assets
3. The sale of existing capital assets
4. Declaration of a corporate dividend

The assumption base developed for a cash flow projection should take all of these items into account. To be completely accurate, this project will require gathering information from others. For example, you may not be in the position to know that the company plans to apply for new loans or finance thousands of dollars in new assets.

The purpose of the cash flow projection is to look for possible problems in the next year and to avoid them through timing and control. For example, your president might plan to seek short-term financing for the purchase of capital assets at the end of summer. But then you will probably be going into a slowdown, and expenses will exceed income for several months. With better timing, the purchase might make more sense in a season when the company's working capital is stronger.

Build your assumption base by documenting every item that will affect cash flow. And be especially aware of timing. For example, one company projecting substantial growth in sales failed to allow a lag time of one to two months for collection of accounts, which distorted cash flow projections.

Use an assumption worksheet such as the one shown in Cash Flow Assumption to develop dependable and complete notes on cash flow (Figure 5-4). Following is an example of how this worksheet can be used:

Figure 5-4

cash flow assumption

Assumption: _____

_____

_____

_____

MONTH	NOTES	SOURCES OF CASH	APPLICATIONS OF CASH
January	___	___	___
February	___	___	___
March	___	___	___
April	___	___	___
May	___	___	___
June	___	___	___
July	___	___	___
August	___	___	___
September	___	___	___
October	___	___	___
November	___	___	___
December	___	___	___

Notes _____

_____

_____

Cash Flow Assumption

Assumption: The company will borrow $140,000 to finance its planned marketing expansion, based on a decision made by the board of directors. This loan is scheduled to occur in March, and will be repaid on a one-year schedule. The monthly payments will be $12,406 (based on 11.5% interest rate assumed), with payments to begin on May 1. (See table.)

Month	Notes	Sources of cash	Applications of cash
January			
February			
March	(1)	$140,000	
April			
May	(2)		$12,406
June			12,406
July			12,406
August			12,406
September			12,406
October			12,406
November			12,406
December	(3)		12,406

Notes:
 (1) $140,000 loan
 (2) Repayments begin, one-year amortization
 (3) Note for next year: repayments will continue from January through April

In this example, the entire note payment is included in the cash flow projection. However, if the budget already includes an estimate of interest, the projection should be adjusted, reporting only the principal portion of each month's payment.

The sources and applications of cash are listed separately, even though the net effect can be easily proven. This is done because sources and applications should be listed separately on the month-to-month projection. This presentation improves clarity and enables management to review the projection with a better understanding of the flow of money.

When assumptions for all matters affecting cash flow have been completed, the actual projections can be constructed and presented for approval. Be sure to consider everything that will affect working capital:

1. Net profits
2. Noncash expenses in the budget
3. Acquisition and disposal of capital assets
4. Increases or decreases in accounts receivable, inventory, and other assets
5. Increases or decreases in accounts and notes payable, as well as other liabilities
6. The effect of existing or planned controls over assets and expenses
7. Additions of paid-in capital
8. Dividend payments, if applicable

The completed projection should begin with the level of cash currently available and carry that forward each month. For example, a cash flow projection for the first quarter might be as shown in the table.

Cash Flow Projection
First Quarter

	January	February	March
Beginning cash balance	$214,650	$23,405	$31,730
Sources of cash:			
Net profit	$110,500	$ 89,000	$ 82,600
Plus: depreciation	13,000	13,000	13,000
Capital asset sales	- 0 -	2,000	- 0 -
Payments rec'd on acct.	16,000	14,000	12,000
Loan proceeds	- 0 -	120,000	- 0 -
Total additions	$139,500	$238,000	$107,600
Applications of cash:			
Payments on notes	$ 16,345	$ 16,345	$ 16,345
Capital asset purchases	6,000	184,000	61,000
Reduction of payables	8,400	29,330	14,080
Dividend payments	300,000	- 0 -	- 0 -
Total applications	$330,745	$229,675	$ 91,425
Ending cash balance	$ 23,405	$ 31,730	$ 47,905

Note that each month's ending cash balance is carried over to the beginning cash balance for the following month. The details of sources and applications should all be supported with a cash flow assumption sheet that (a) explains the assumption and source of information and (b) indicates which months will be affected.

Looking back to the first quarter example, what will happen if the projection goes forward and includes a cash payment in April for new capital assets? If the projected cash goes into the negative, the company must take action now to plan for this problem. Recommend that management consider the following steps:

1. Take out a new loan to offset the anticipated shortage
2. Delay the purchase of capital assets
3. Reduce future dividend payments
4. Reevaluate planned debt payments, perhaps seeking financing for a longer term

The purpose of cash flow projecting is to ensure that adequate cash will be available to operate throughout the year. The availability of working capital is essential to operations—meaning the need for control over current assets and liabilities and the careful planning, use, and reserving of cash balances.

Just as variance reports are prepared for income forecasts and expense budgets, they should be planned for cash flow projections. Only by watching and adjusting on a monthly basis will you and your organization be able to ensure that adequate cash reserves are on hand when needed.

WHEN CASH FLOW IS NEGATIVE

You prepare cash flow projections to spot potential trouble in the future, control negative trends, and ensure that a planned program is maintained. But there may be instances when the projection shows that you will, in fact, go into the red.

In projecting the future, it is easy to make it all come out all right—on paper, at least. But be aware that altering your projection to avoid this problem is not always a good idea. If your basic assumptions are sound, look instead for alternatives, and point out potential problems to management.

One company was planning a major market expansion for the new year, which included opening several new offices (meaning overhead commitments, capital assets, and high travel expenses, all in advance of income being generated). But upon reviewing cash flow projections, it became obvious the company could not afford to move as quickly as it had originally planned.

In the first round of reviews, one manager suggested raising the income assumptions in new markets, so that cash flow projections would remain above zero. To some extent this idea was not entirely unreasonable. If, in fact, the generation of income could be achieved by setting specific goals for new branch offices, it was considered possible that a more aggressive and optimistic approach could be taken. But the timing factor had to be considered as well, regardless of the level of future income.

The company would have to open offices, fund advance travel and lease commitments, and buy furniture and equipment. The problem was not so much in estimating how much income would result from opening new offices, but one of what the company would be able to afford *before* that income hit the books. From a starting date, it would be two to three months before income would be received in cash.

As a result of this review, the company had to schedule its planned expansion over a longer period of time. If it had higher cash balances available, an aggressive expansion plan might have been practicable. But the reality of limited cash brought the realization that achieving profitable growth would take longer. The company might have been able to stick to the original plan by seeking new financing. But management recognized the risk of going into new territory. Expanding with debt financing would have been too great a chance to take, making the company's cash position even more precarious.

Chances are you're not authorized to make major decisions regarding dividend payments, commitments to outside financing, or the purchase and sale of capital assets. But use the information you have to point out opportunities to management as part of the budget process. If you are able to identify potential problems in the future and offer practical solutions to them, that makes your work valuable and significant. And that should be the purpose of the budgeting process—to use all available information to anticipate the near-term future and suggest a course of action.

WORK PROJECT

1. As part of a cash flow control program, one company tracks the current ratio each month. There is no seasonal variation to consider. For the first four months of the year, the following figures are tracked:

Month	Current assets	Current liabilities
January	$216,480	$101,600
February	244,160	120,905
March	238,933	121,680
April	251,350	128,607

What is the current ratio each month, and what is the direction of the trend? Name three possible contributing factors.

2. You are instructed to develop a cash flow projection for the coming year. Name four types of information to include in developing a reasonable assumption base.

3. Identify five possible modifications that can be made to this year's cash flow projection to offset an anticipated negative cash situation.

6

Putting It All Together

A sick man that gets talking about himself, a woman that gets talking about her baby, and an author that begins reading out of his own book, never know when to stop.

—Oliver Wendell Holmes, Sr.

A department manager was observed leaving work each day with the thick companywide budget report. His boss commended him for his diligence, but expressed concern than he might be working too hard. "Oh, I'm not working on the budget," the manager said. "I've been reading it in bed each night as a cure for my insomnia."

Budget processes often get out of control. By the time you're ready to report on the status of a budget from one month to another, so much paper is involved that you either overwhelm others with complexity or simply can't answer questions. Unfortunately, a good number of managers make budget presentations that are ultimately self-defeating. But even with copious information to compile and report, you *can* put together an all-inclusive and readable report.

A large report can be overwhelming. Imagine a group of executives filing into the meeting room for a monthly budget report to face a bound document the size of the New York Yellow Pages. It would take at least a week to read through all the detailed analysis, study the trend charts, and pore over the worksheets. You have answered every possible question that could be asked about the budget in this report, so as not to be put on the spot with an embarrassing challenge. The only problem is that it would be nearly impossible to find that information quickly.

A disorganized budget report is no better and may be even more common than the overlong report. Typically managers prepare a brief report on the budget to present at the meeting. During the review, one of the members of the committee asks what's in the budget for a particular expense. The disorganized presenter refers to the mountain of files on his lap—which contain the original, first and second revisions, worksheets, memos, and other paperwork on the budget—trying in vain to find the answer. After a few minutes of delay, he admits defeat but promises to get back with the information later. Meanwhile his boss makes a silent note for the pending salary review.

THE MOST EFFICIENT WAY

When you're truly organized beforehand the report waiting at each place around the conference table is wafer thin. At first, the budget review committee members think you don't have the report. But in summarized form, it's all there—a one-page breakdown between actual and budget, cross-referenced to brief explanations of all significant variances. During the meeting, questions arise about the budget. You flip open a binder to promptly give the answer.

The budget report that ultimately goes to your supervisor, the company's president, or a budget review committee should be as brief as possible. (See "Formats for Variance Reports" in the next chapter.) Ideally, the entire picture can be summarized on one page, showing the budget, actual and variance, for each category of income, expense, and cash flow. But backing up that short report must be all the information necessary to answer questions.

Become the expert on the budget, its variances and assumptions. Think of budgeting as a grouping of information sources. You have the extremely abbreviated version (the report), backed up by original assumptions, and further supported by your detailed worksheets and analyses.

ORGANIZING THE FILE

After you complete your final budget, organize your file and put all the worksheets and documents together in one place. This will prove to be the only way to stay in control throughout the year, when you'll be explaining variances to your supervisor and perhaps to several other executives in meetings.

Do not include worksheets made obsolete by subsequent changes, but keep documentation of the process for the entire budget period (and throw it away the following year). Place the analysis paperwork in a binder with all the other material necessary to present and support your budget. You'll refer to the information in this binder throughout the year, not only for variance reporting but also to examine original assumptions and identify the causes of problems in specific accounts.

Include the following in your organization binder:

1. Detailed analysis. Include the actual worksheets you used to develop your budget, whether they analyze activity in an account during the previous period, summarize projected information supplied by another department, or study seasonal variations. Specify the assumption on which you have based your approach. You may use the worksheet in Figure 6-1 when part of your budget is based on analysis of account activity.

2. Budget worksheets. For each account of income, expense, or cash flow, prepare a single sheet that summarizes the budget and cross-references it by component (a component being one of the sources for building your budget). Use a worksheet like the one shown in Figure 6-2.

    For example, the components of an advertising expense budget might consist of newspaper, direct mail, radio, and magazine assumptions. Each of these is listed by month, and a total computed, along with brief explanations of each (cross-referenced to detailed analysis sheets).

3. Final budget. Place the final, complete budget on a single worksheet (or break it down by quarters or into six-month sections). See the example in Figure 6-3.

Figure 6-1

detailed analysis

Account _____ Date _____

For the period _____ through _____

Assumptions

Analysis

MONTH

explanation

Figure 6–2

budget worksheet

Account _____ Date _____

For the period _____ through _____

C O M P O N E N T S

Month	(1)	(2)	(3)	(4)	Total
_____	_____	_____	_____	_____	_____
_____	_____	_____	_____	_____	_____
_____	_____	_____	_____	_____	_____
_____	_____	_____	_____	_____	_____
_____	_____	_____	_____	_____	_____
_____	_____	_____	_____	_____	_____

Explanation

(1) _____

_____

(2) _____

_____

(3) _____

_____

(4) _____

_____

Figure 6-3

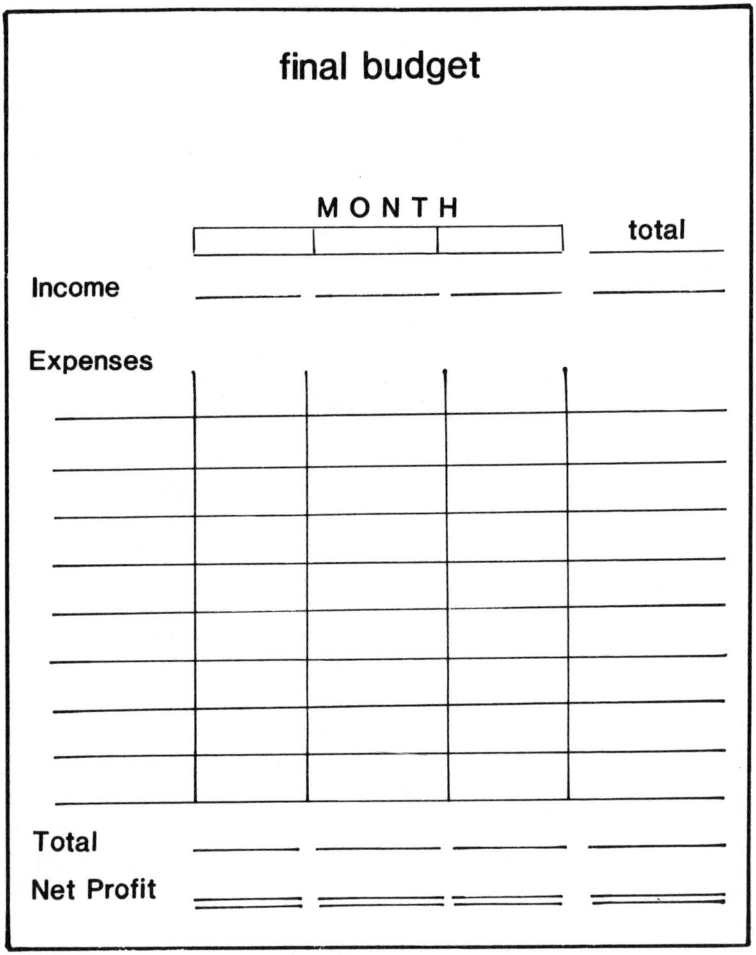

final budget

	MONTH			total
Income				
Expenses				
Total				
Net Profit				

In this case, the income forecast and expense budget are summarized in the format of a profit and loss statement. Each month has its own column, with a total for the period being reported. Include an additional sheet for the cash flow projection, also with one column for each month.

Organize the back-up to allow quick access to the needed level of detail. For example, during a budget review meeting, an executive asks for the components of the advertising budget. You open your binder to the "expenses" section, find the advertising budget worksheet, and give a breakdown. If more information is needed, turn the page and explain the detailed analysis and assumptions that make up that component of the budget.

If this seems like a lot of work to organize a budget file, remember that there is no other way to handle such a massive amount of paperwork, and you can't know in advance what kinds of questions will be asked. Be fully prepared to justify and explain anything that involves the budget report and all your gathered details.

With a complete package arranged for ease of access in a pressure situation (like a budget review meeting), you can present brief, concise reports free of unwanted details, and still answer any challenge that comes your way.

AT THE BUDGET MEETING

Nothing is more impressive than seeing someone at a meeting who is completely prepared, who shows a thorough ability to organize, has a grasp of the topic, and is not afraid to interpret facts and make recommendations.

It is impressive because it is rare. You have probably observed a general laziness and sense of apathy, a lack of personal involvement among many of the people who attend meetings. Lack of preparation or comprehension may not be taken as a reflection on the individual, but it should. Your career will be successful if you observe this rule: Never go to a meeting unprepared.

For example, the manager of a three-department floor attended a monthly budget review meeting, and had to give a report. It showed the actual results year-to-date, the budget, and variances. Everything was summarized on one sheet, with needed explanations cross-referenced to between three and five attached pages. Anyone interested in knowing the cause of a variance could look it up right in the report.

That's all the manager presented. But she had much more than that at the meeting. In a looseleaf binder were the following materials, each in its own indexed section:

1. Each month's budget report
2. The original, final forecast, budget, and cash flow projection
3. Worksheets for income forecasts

4. Worksheets for expense budgets, arranged in the same order as presented on the variance report
5. Worksheets for cash flow projections, also presented in the same order as the report
6. Notes taken during monthly budget review meetings each month, including questions asked and action decisions

The greater your organization, the more easily you will be able to answer questions. This is especially true for accounts with several complex components or assumptions.

For example, for your income forecast you develop three major assumptions and several different components:

1. Recruiting assumptions
    number of new recruits
    attrition of new recruits
    attrition of existing sales force
2. Production assumptions
    averages, new recruits
    averages, existing sales force
    seasonal adjustments
3. New service centers
    marketing expansion
    timing of new production

All of this will involve gathering of information on worksheets, analyzing average recruiting and production trends in the past, and estimating how the future will differ. So when you find yourself reporting a 13% unfavorable variance a few months later, what can you say when an executive asks you, "What's in that forecast?"

With complete organization you will understand where the assumption has strayed. Perhaps the number of new recruits is below estimates, or their production takes longer than expected to come in. Or the averages for the existing sales force are lower than the trend indicated. Or the marketing expansion plan has been delayed. Chances are, a combination of these factors caused the problem.

A complex assumption base (or, a series of assumptions) will be especially difficult to pin down with a simple answer. But you will have the answers and be able to give them promptly, even to the extent of showing how a combination of factors contributes to the variance. You might discover, for example, that only 70% of the number of estimated new recruits have actually come to the company, that their production average is lower than the forecast, and that the unexpected loss of some high volume salespeople has brought down the average for the existing sales force.

Anticipate questions about large unfavorable variances, and prepare in advance of the meeting. Pay special attention to those accounts involving complex assumptions and prepare a supplemental analysis. This supplement need not be included in the budget report unless everyone will need to see it. But have the analysis in hand, including sufficient copies.

Volunteer information when the discussion reaches the account. Draw attention to the unfavorable variance and distribute your analysis. Budget review committees are used to hearing vague answers to questions and to dealing with ill-prepared presenters. Rise above that average by anticipating their needs and by taking a direct approach. By using this technique you can expect action that otherwise could not be taken for lack of information.

For example, several factors contributing to an unfavorable variance in income might lead management to decide that recruiting has to be improved, that incentives must be developed to increase existing average production levels, or that a delayed marketing expansion plan must be brought up to schedule immediately.

REPORTING WITHOUT DIRECT REVIEW

The communication techniques explained above will help to improve management's perception of you as an employee. Your competence, preparation, and diligence will be recognized when you present clear information and back it up. But how should you deal with the same issues if your company doesn't hold a monthly budget review meeting?

Some organizations opt to distribute a report without meeting regularly to discuss it among executives and managers. This is unfortunate because proper use of the budget demands action. A negative trend demands corrective response, and that can only occur when people meet and assignments are made.

Keeping a report simple and still being prepared to answer questions is difficult if you write your report and send it through the internal mail. In the typical company, you would be unlikely to ever hear a response to your budget summary. And surely no one will take corrective action.

Of course, not having to present your conclusions to a roomful of executives simplifies your job. Budget presentations are intimidating, even for experienced and knowledgeable employees. But the lack of direct communication means the entire budgeting process is going unused.

You can take several steps to deal with a situation in which little or no interaction is involved in budget reporting:

1. Recommend to your supervisor that a direct review meeting be held each month, to make decisions about how to reverse negative variances, and to give appropriate assignments.
2. Include a supplemental report with your budget that includes recommendations for action. Discuss this idea with your supervisor, being careful to not put yourself in a position beyond the scope of your authority.
3. Suggest procedures for assigning action in response to discovered unfavorable variances. In those cases where the variance is caused by current conditions (rather than the result of inaccurate budgeting), immediate action *should* be taken.

Your position will be difficult, unrewarding, and frustrating if you are responsible for reporting on the budget but lack the authority or position to direct or suggest action. By making recommendations to your supervisor for procedural changes, you can eventually change a poorly organized system. Suggest changes you would make, if given the authority, that would prevent or reverse negative trends, cut expenses, and improve profits.

Organize the paperwork that went into making the budget and be prepared to verify conclusions you will draw during the year. Test assumptions and either validate the budget or show where it fails. Then you will be seen as a capable and diligent employee. Don't lose sight of the budget's ultimate purpose—to control and create a range of financial events in the near future. Consider a final budget as the indicator of management's expectations, and measure everything against that. And remember that the report itself is not the end product. It's only a tool to communicate valuable information.

WORK PROJECT

1. You are working on the detailed analysis for your department's travel expense budget. What are some of the likely assumptions that will go into this analysis?

2. The budget for printing expenses next year includes the following: $850 per month for the company newsletter; estimated March and August expenses for new letterhead, averaging $1,200 each time; and other printing that has averaged $475 per month in the past, with an expected 5% increase in July. How will you fill out a budget worksheet to show these different components?

3. Organize an assumption summary for an account with the following: recurring monthly expense starting out at $550 and expected to grow 3% each month; payments in March, June, and October of $4,000 each; and expenses estimated at $385 for the first four months, a 10% increase in the fifth month, and another 5% increase starting in the ninth month.

7

Surviving the Variance Blues

I have only one eye. What do you want me to watch, the speedometer or the road?

—Moshe Dayan

Two managers walked together on their way to a monthly budget review meeting. "I'm a little nervous," one admitted. "My department is over budget, and they'll expect me to make up the difference, but I don't know where the money will come from." As they approached the door to the meeting room, the other manager advised, "Keep one hand on your wallet."

All that work you do to validate assumptions and support the numbers you develop is only the beginning of the budgeting process. The real test of a budget's value comes in the comparison to actual expenses. Then you find out how well you looked ahead, and whether or not problems can be identified and solved during the year.

Most companies prepare a monthly report that lists actual and budget, highlighting variances. The report includes a brief comment, and as long as the explanation reads convincingly, that's the end of the discussion. But the variance report can be so much more. It can be used as a means for proposing concrete solutions rather than merely describing the variance.

This reasoning can be applied to any problem. For example, at a school open house, the teacher informs you that your child's grades are slipping. The reason, it seems, is that she's not doing homework assignments.

Are you content with merely identifying the reason for the problem? Of course not. You will now want to take corrective action, making sure homework gets done every day. Your measures might include restrictions on television, direct supervision, and direct help if needed with the assignments.

This commonsense approach should also be applied to your company's budgeting process. But as often as not, identifying and explaining problems is considered sufficient. You can adopt two attitudes about budget reports. You can come up with a reasonable explanation of variances that satisfies the review committee and get off the hook. Or you can see budgeting as an opportunity to propose action to correct problems.

Your budgeting procedure—or, more to the point, your attitude about the procedure—should include a search for effective solutions. Set standards for yourself and your department, striving to always show management where expenses can be cut (through controls and other actions), where profits can be increased, and where positive trends can be encouraged. Think of the reporting of budget variances not as a problem, but as an opportunity to provide guidance to management (see "Budgeting Standards").

Budgeting Standards

1. Prepare comparison reports every month.
2. Include precise identification of problems and recommendations for corrective action.
3. Managers overseeing the reporting process should ensure that variance explanations are correct and that actual results are not manipulated to conform to the budget.
4. Throughout the month, make all employees aware of budgetary limits and goals.
5. Analyze variances and use them to prepare more accurate budgets in the future.

VARIANCE REPORT FORMAT

The goal in formatting a variance report is to present information as clearly as possible. The reviewer should be able to see where variances have occurred, and should be able to easily find answers to obvious questions those variances create: Why did they occur? and What's being done to correct the problem?

Start by determining which numbers to report: monthly or year-to-date. A good case can be made either way, although experience shows that year-to-date reporting is better for several reasons.

Some variances result strictly from the timing of bookings and invoicing. For example, one company budgeted $40,000 for the cost of its annual CPA audit. The expense was estimated to fall in February, with billing in March. Accruing the expense would have been possible but company policy was that expenses were not to be booked until statements or invoices had been received. A monthly report showed a high favorable variance, but the explanation read:

> This was budgeted in February, but to date, we have not been billed. This variance will be absorbed in March.

Reporting only on the monthly variances could allow large discrepancies to fall through the cracks. A problem this month will not show up again on next month's report, even if it's still a problem. An advantage of year-to-date reporting is that it brings up existing problems every month, reminding management that a problem exists between the budget and actual results. If the current problem is only a temporary timing difference, it will disappear the following month.

The best way to structure the monthly report is to always compare year-to-date results. Elements of variances related to past months should be noted and referenced back to the previous month, with new variance elements commented upon separately. For example, a variance explanation could read:

> The variance of $4,852 includes $3,150 incurred in earlier months for unbudgeted expenses, and $1,702 in the current month.

This is not an adequate explanation. A good explanation would compare assumptions to actual expenditures.

The variance report should include a breakdown of all accounts in the same format as the company's income statement. The cover page is a summary of the numbers and refers to a narrative section for explanations. Following this are listings of the actual and budget numbers, then the amount of variance and the percentage of the variance. The monthly variance report format is shown in Figure 7-1.

The percentage of variance should reflect the amount that actual results are above or below the budget. For example, travel expenses were budgeted year-to-date at \$34,800 but actual expenses were \$38,063. To compute the variance percentage:

$$\$38,063 - \$34,800 = \$3,263$$
$$\$\ 3,263 \div \$34,800 = (9.4\%)$$

Figure 7-1

variance report

Date _____

ACCOUNT	REF.	YEAR-TO-DATE			%
		ACTUAL	BUDGET	VARIANCE	

A typical breakdown of the variance report looks like this:

Account	Ref	Actual	Budget	Variance	%
Income	1	$318,800	$300,000	$18,800	6.3
Travel	2	38,063	34,800	(3,263)	(9.4)
Telephone		11,335	11,250		
Office		6,837	6,500		

The summary proceeds through each account in the same manner. Note the references to the next section of the report which gives actual explanations.

Report favorable as well as unfavorable variances. This breakdown, for example, shows a 6.3% favorable variance in income. A favorable variance may indicate a problem, just as does an unfavorable variance. For example, why was income underestimated? Perhaps because of overly conservative budgeting assumptions, a seasonal variance, or a problem in the way that income is being budgeted (versus the way it actually enters the books). Considering the importance of cash flow to the company, diligent effort should track down the causes of favorable variances.

Unfavorable variances and their percentages are always reported in parentheses. Note that "unfavorable" means expenses exceed the budget or, in the case of income, the forecast amount exceeds the actual amount.

In the example above, telephone and office accounts are not reported, even though small variances did occur. Rarely are budgets and actual results identical, but a slight degree of variance need not be reported. Recommend a policy that sets a cut-off point for requiring a variance explanation. A sample of such a policy statement is the following:

> All significant variances, favorable or unfavorable, will require an explanation. A "significant" variance is one that meets these tests:
>
> (a) The amount of variance is $500 or more; and
> (b) The percentage of the variance is 5% or more away from the forecast or budgeted amount.

The actual amounts and percentages should be adjusted based on the volume of business in the company. For gross income under $20 million, a $500/5%

cut-off may be appropriate. But if the gross is in the hundreds of millions or in billions of dollars, use a higher cut-off amount. Or adjust the amount and leave the percentage intact. For example, significant variance might meet the test of $2,000 or 5% away from budget.

The variance report should also be used for reporting cash flow status. Use the same format and prepare the report on a year-to-date basis, in the same manner as reporting for income and expenses.

As the year progresses, reporting on a year-to-date basis can become tedious, especially if you have broken out your budget in monthly totals. For example, by the fifth month, you must add five lines for every account. To make the job easier and to maintain absolute control over the math, when the final budget is approved prepare a summary of the year-to-date numbers in each account.

Following is a sample of a monthly income forecast and total expense budget:

Monthly Budget

Month	Income	Expenses	Net
Jan	$ 485,000	$ 452,000	$ 33,000
Feb	510,000	480,000	30,000
Mar	495,000	461,000	34,000
Apr	495,000	457,000	38,000
May	505,000	482,000	23,000
Jun	525,000	488,000	37,000
Total	$3,015,000	$2,820,000	$195,000

A year-to-date budget should, of course, include the details of every account. But to show how this budget works, it could be rearranged:

Year-to-Date-Budget

Month	Income	Expenses	Net
Jan	$ 485,000	$ 452,000	$ 33,000
Feb	995,000	932,000	63,000
Mar	1,490,000	1,393,000	97,000
Apr	1,985,000	1,850,000	135,000
May	2,490,000	2,332,000	158,000
Jun	3,015,000	2,820,000	195,000

This is not a time-consuming chart to build, yet it guarantees the accuracy of your math. Note that cross-checking the net profit amount to the month-to-month addition verifies the year-to-date totals. From this worksheet it is easy to place year-to-date budget and forecast totals on the variance report.

The year-to-date format will be the best in most cases. But in some accounts, especially those involving complex transactions, a variance might consist of several different factors. Some will relate to the current month, others will be carried forward from the past. In this case, take the analysis a step further and break the variance into different parts.

Figure 7-2 shows how to do this breakdown. For example, travel and entertainment expenses might show a variance made up of the following:

1. Timing problems, with air tickets paid a month in advance of a planned trip.
2. Lower than expected budget levels for certain executives.
3. Budget assumptions made by an individual for some types of T+E, and a mixture of positive and negative variances.

In such a case, the variance analysis helps the explanation considerably. The budget refers the reader to a narrative section. That section contains an additional reference to the variance analysis worksheet.

THE EXPLANATION SECTION

Following the summary sheet is the explanation section. To help the reviewer avoid flipping pages, begin each explanation with a summary of actual and budget totals, and the variance. A typical explanation section will look like this:

```
Ref
 1  INCOME
        Year-to-date              $318,800
        Budget                     300,000
        Variance                  $ 18,800    6.3%
```

The forecast assumption called for new recruit production to average $3,200 per month and to be booked three months after hire date.

Figure 7-2

variance analysis

Date _____

	ACTUAL RESULTS	BUDGET ASSUMPTIONS	VARIANCE	%
I: Prior year–to–date				
_____				
_____				
_____				
_____				
Total				
II: Current month				
_____				
_____				
_____				
_____				
Total				

This assumption was overly conservative in many respects. We have recruited 22% more new salespeople than anticipated. Production has averaged $3,850 per month, and has been booked within two months from hire date.

It should be noted that production levels for the existing sales force are falling behind the forecast by approximately 8%. However, this unfavorable condition is not expected to continue. Branch offices are operating on the basis of individual production goals, and current month volume is higher than the average as of this report's date.

2 TRAVEL

Year-to-date	$38,063	
Budget	34,800	
Variance	($ 3,263)	(9.4%)

This variation consists of several elements (see attached variance report). Significant unfavorable conditions include spending in excess of estimates for executive airfare and hotel bills, and prepayment of site fees for a meeting next month.

A portion of this variance ($2,100) was originally budgeted for the next two months and is expected to be absorbed. The balance is expected to remain in variance with the budget throughout the year. The budget did not anticipate as heavy a travel schedule for executives.

Types of Explanations

Note that in each case the explanation is tied into the assumption base. This tells the reviewer exactly what went wrong, and why. That specificity will help improve the forecasting and budgeting process in the following year, and also tells management what actions, if any, should be taken.

In the case of travel expenses, for example, the president of the company could react by instructing other traveling executives to obtain approval before making a commitment to a trip; or the president might simply accept the variance and allow a budget revision.

Should you be content with a complete explanation of the underlying causes of variances? No. That only identifies the problem. The purpose of identification is to provide a basis for proposing solutions.

Do not expect someone else to interpret your variance explanations and independently determine the proper course of action. While some talented executives are able to do this, many would review your budget report passively. They consider an understanding of reasons sufficient.

Conclude your variance explanation with a comment falling into one of these areas:

1. The variance is a timing difference and will disappear in coming months. No action is required.
2. The basic assumption in the budget was wrong, as proven by what is being spent. The budget should be revised.
3. Spending is not being controlled. Action is necessary now to eliminate the unfavorable trend.

Include recommendations when the second or third conditions are present. An example of a possible comment to include for a revision is the following:

> The assumption used in our current budget did not allow for this expense. Due to a recently implemented marketing plan not anticipated at the end of last year, the company is spending more on travel than is allowed for in the budget.
>
> It is recommended that a revision be made to the budget to reflect a more realistic future spending level.

An example of an explanation when spending is not being controlled:

> Travel expenses are exceeding the level established by historical trends. The budget was developed based upon individual travel plans, and is still realistic within the context of our marketing plan.
>
> It is recommended that all travel expenses should be approved in advance of commitment, that we should request discount fare arrangements through our travel agent, and that exact travel budgets should be imposed on an individual basis.

For more guidance, see "Using Tact in Recommendations."

In cases where a variance proves the assumption base was wrong, the company will have to accept an unanticipated spending level. In that event, recommend a revision to the budget.

Using Tact in Recommendations

One potential problem in recommending a tightening of controls is that those with more power than you often are at fault. How can you suggest tightening the reins without making enemies?

Never name names when recommending controls. Avoid assigning the blame, and base your suggestion strictly on approved budgets. By suggesting that the budget should be followed, emphasize saving money by reducing expenses. No one wants to put his name on a document that criticizes others. Compare the following recommendations:

To Avoid	*Alternative*
The vice president of marketing has exceeded the entertainment budget every month.	All departments should be required to stay within budgets for entertainment expenses.
Executives should not be allowed to spend money for travel without first obtaining permission from the president.	A new procedure is proposed, calling for preapproval by the president of all travel expenses above $100.

Figure 7-3 shows a form for this purpose. Complete this form whenever conditions show the current budget to be incorrect. The account and date are written in at the top (the date being the latest month-end), then the condition is summarized. Following this is a brief explanation of the problem and a recommendation for a new budget level.

Always include a proposed revised assumption with the request. If the company's policy is to revise budgets every six months (the most common procedure), the request can be made in advance and then held until that point. But with a severe problem the change should be allowed at once.

If you do revise your budget before a planned revision date, be sure to incorporate that change in your budget package. That means incorporating the revised assumption, details, and changes to the summary sheet, and a corrected year-to-date budget summary (to be used in preparing variance reports).

The first month after a change, include a comment on the variance report. By revising the budget, you eliminate the variance, so track that

Figure 7–3

request for budget revision

Account _____ Date _____

    YEAR–TO–DATE ACTUAL $ _____

    YEAR–TO–DATE BUDGET $ _____

    VARIANCE $ _____ ___ %

The cause of this variance is: _____

_____

_____

_____

_____

_____

The budget should be changed to: _____

_____

_____

_____

_____ Effective date _____

(Attach revised assumptions)

Approved _____

Title _____ Date _____

change in a comment. For example, your explanation the first month might read:

> The year-to-date condition shows no significant variance, due to a revision in the budget.
>   Last month's variance was unfavorable by 28%, due to expenditures for (. . . explanation . . .). A revision was approved and incorporated into the budget during the past month. (See attached revised assumption).

With a solid set of assumptions, a consistent and clear monthly variance reporting system, and a means for recommending action, your budget procedure will become a valuable one. It will save your company money by reducing current expenses and anticipating the future. And that's the essence of good budgeting—making it a control tool rather than just a mechanical process.

WORK PROJECT

1. Compute the amount of variance for the following accounts, indicate whether they are favorable or unfavorable, and figure the percentage of variance.

Account	Actual	Budget
Income	$886,703	$846,750
Travel	42,855	38,300
Entertainment	9,010	10,000
Office supplies	10,861	10,400

2. Your definition of a "significant" variance is any amount that is $500 or more away from budget and 5% higher or lower. On this basis, which of the variances in the first problem meet your test?

3. Your year-to-date budget for meetings and conventions includes $18,450 in May. As of the end of May, only $6,200 of that total was paid, caus-ing a large favorable variance. How should this be explained in your variance report?

8

Creating a Profit Center

*Some circumstantial evidence is very strong,
as when you find a trout in the milk.*

—Henry David Thoreau

*An employee suggested to the manager that some depart-
mental expenses could be reduced if controls were put into
place. "I don't have time to develop controls," the manager responded. "We're going to be tied up for the next month on budget revisions."*

Just getting through a budget and finally achieving approval is so exhaust-
ing that many people think the job is done for another year and they men-
tally put it away. But this is actually the point where the budget can be put to
good use. Now that you have sound assumptions and a strong standard for
the coming months, it's important to see it through, to look for evidence of
trends, and to get them under control.

TAKING ACTION

The typical variance report is prepared each month and distributed to several managers and executives. In some companies, the group that receives the report is called the finance committee. In others, only vice presidents and other executives get copies. Or every manager may receive the report. Rarely, however, are actions taken in response to the information revealed.

The reasons for nonresponse include a lack of understanding of the entire process and its real intention, poor variance explanations that distract from the real problem, or a budgeting process that is not based on detailed assumptions.

With an established assumption base and monthly reports tied in to it, your control tool is in hand. The next step is to decide on appropriate actions.

In some companies, actually *using* the budget is a new idea. Rather than trying to cut expenses or control cash flow, some managers and executives only misuse the budget. For example, upon reviewing an employee's performance, they often say, "We can't give you a pay increase, because there's no money in the budget."

Statements like that imply that the budget is being used and followed strictly. The employee can hardly argue with or challenge the claim because it sounds so final. But in fact, the budget is rarely given that much importance and is used only as an excuse.

No one is really fooled by the no-money-in-the-budget tactic; most of us know exactly how little budgeting is really used in our own organizations. Actually using budget information involves examples like the following:

1. Recommending a new control procedure to monitor and reduce expenses directly.
2. Identifying unnecessary spending.
3. Anticipating a risk of excessive spending in the future, based upon unexpected increases in revenue to counteract the tendency to overspend when revenues are rising.

How can *you* change the way your company operates? You may not be in a position to set policy, or to change a long-standing procedure of passive response to the budget. But to influence the way your company uses its budgets take the following action steps:

1. Recommend review and response procedures that incorporate a sound assumption base in budgeting.
2. Show by example how effectively controls can be developed, implemented, and used to actually save money.
3. Include action suggestions in your variance explanations and follow them up with additional internal requests for response.

FORMS OF CONTROL

Controls may be designed for your department alone (as part of a departmental or a companywide budget), or even for the entire organization.

Your being able to put companywide controls into place might seem unlikely if you are isolated in a single department; you might not have the rank to impose controls on others; and suggesting change is always a sensitive issue that might be poorly received by other employees and managers.

Each of these problems can be overcome. In one data processing company, the manager of the customer service department revised several forms and cut ten hours a week from paperwork, filing, and other clerical functions. The move also freed up file space. She wanted to suggest that similar changes would cut expenses in other departments, but didn't have the authority to make the suggestion directly. Her solution: She prepared a report explaining the approach she used to evaluate paperwork efficiency, and submitted it to her supervisor with a recommendation to distribute it to every manager in the company. That was done, and several other departments were also able to cut expenses. A successful case history is always the most compelling argument in favor of change.

Controls can include new procedures. You can put several forms of control into effect in your own department, or recommend them on a companywide basis, including:

1. Setting rules to control internal meetings, including preparation of a specific agenda, limiting attendance to only those who must be present, enforcing a strict start and stop time, and doing away with disruptions.
2. Using a diligent travel agency to prearrange travel for executives, including advance reservations (to get discount fares), clustering out-

of-town meetings to reduce the number of trips, and joining airline mileage clubs to discount future travel.

3. Creating centralized responsibility for outside printing, including price comparisons, combination jobs for discounted total costs, and an approval system to ensure the best ordering and pricing policies.

4. Setting limitations on the use of delivery services. Overnight delivery rates are often paid unnecessarily. And due to lack of coordination, some branch offices may be receiving several mailings per day. Centralizing and coordinating outgoing delivery cuts expenses and the number of mailings made.

5. Eliminating paperwork. A review of internal forms may reveal that several procedures are time consuming and out of date. For example, one company found a form in use that consisted of an original and five carbon copies. Only one copy was usually needed. This form was replaced with a cheaper two-part form that could be supplemented by a photocopy when needed. Many other forms in use were obsolete as the result of automation in the company, and were eliminated.

Any one of these ideas can be generated in response to discovered variances. It is difficult to suggest new procedures when there isn't a problem, and you can be perceived as a bureaucrat if you make a suggestion without a current crisis. But when there is a problem, there's also a compelling motive to find a solution.

THE CONTROL ANALYSIS

Another form of control is the simple analysis of accounts, which should be achieved on a comparative basis. List on a worksheet the elements in an account on a monthly and year-to-date basis and compare these to the assumptions in the budget.

This process reveals faults in assumptions, which helps you to make better assumptions in the future. It also points out possible problems in the near future, before a variance becomes significant. Use a form like the one shown in Figure 8-1.

The analysis can be quite simple. Just look at what has gone into the account and comment appropriately. Having this analysis in hand adds sup-

Figure 8–1

---

control analysis

Account _____ Month _____

	REF.	ACTUAL	BUDGET	VARIANCE
Prior year-to-date				
Current month				
_____	A			
_____	B			
_____	C			
_____	D			
Total this month				
Total year-to-date				

Notes:

A _____
   _____
   _____

B _____
   _____
   _____

C _____
   _____
   _____

D _____
   _____
   _____

port to your later recommendation for new control procedures. Spotting trends in variances demonstrates your ability to use the budget in the best possible way.

Some accounts do not require analysis. Rent, for example, is set by contract, so reducing it to a worksheet is redundant and without purpose. Concentrate analysis on problem accounts or on accounts where variances are most likely to occur such as office supplies, travel, entertainment, printing expenses, and others with a high volume of transactions.

How can an expense analysis cut variances? In one company an analysis of delivery expense revealed a growing volume of charges without a substantial increase in markets. Analysis revealed that some managers were increasing usage of outside services, leading to the conclusion that better controls were needed.

The same benefits will be found in analyzing for trends in other accounts. Are subscription charges on the rise, and why? Is entertainment expense climbing and exceeding budget? Who is ordering supplies and from which suppliers? Account analysis is not simply listing what's in the account but requires investigation to reveal valid information. Discover what is occurring, pinpoint problems, and then suggest solutions.

How much time should this analysis take? Concentrating on problem accounts reduces the chore to a few isolated areas. This analysis should be completed in less than a half day a month. If you need more time delegate whenever possible.

The manager of a data processing department solved his company's problem with subscriptions. During a monthly budget review meeting, a large unfavorable variance was reported in this account. He wrote up a brief description of the controls he had put in effect in his own department and submitted this to his boss. His simple control required preapproval of all subscriptions ordered by members of his department. Before this procedure no centralized control existed, departmentally or otherwise. The idea was put into effect on a centralized basis, which brought expense under control.

INCOME AND GOAL SETTING

Just as expense controls can increase profits, the properly used forecast can serve as a blueprint for the control of volume.

Many organizations have discovered that rapidly increasing sales levels can also mean lower profits. This results from a tendency to spend excessively, to overcommit to leases, the level of hirings, and other fixed overhead, and a loss in quality that means an eventual loss of customers.

A forecast can control the timing and level of growth to ensure quality in customer service and control over related expenses. This is generally a concern for the highest levels in the company, but a manager participating in the budget review process can help provide information and even suggest control actions.

In one company, a middle-level manager observed that income was outpacing the forecast by more than 40%. Because of this, management was not concerned with several significant unfavorable variances in expenses. But the manager pointed out that many of those conditions were occurring in fixed overhead areas. For example, the company hired a number of new employees, which crowded the existing office space. Additional space was leased in the same building, which created an unfavorable variance in the rent expense account, since the move was not anticipated when the budget was prepared. If the new volume proved to be only temporary or seasonal, the long-term rent commitment would become a serious problem.

As a result of this observation, management agreed to proceed with some caution. It avoided long-term commitments beyond those already made. Income levels were, in fact, seasonal, and did not continue to climb as they had during the early part of the year.

Income forecasts can be used in other ways, too. In companies that depend on a sales force for volume, the forecast should be built upon assumptions made on historical levels, combined with future recruiting and new volume estimates. Then the forecast can be used to build individual goals.

In one organization, the forecast was developed on the basis of historical production. Each sales representative was given an individual goal to match his or her previous production record. For new recruits, minimum goals were set and tracked.

Whenever a salesperson's production fell below this goal, the sales manager was informed, and he helped the person meet and maintain the standard. This standard was also used as a means for evaluating salespeople. Because many representatives exceeded their previous production levels, the collective income forecast was reached.

CASH FLOW CONTROLS

Directly related to income is the need for careful cash flow controls. These controls take many forms, including debt management and tracking of accounts receivable levels. Using the income forecast as a sales goal tool is an effective technique. Because the forecast is built on the basis of individual production, it can also be broken down in the same way. Variances then can be traced to individuals.

In one book publishing house, a similar technique was used for acquisitions editors. Forecasts were tied specifically to book projects each of the editors brought in to the company. Forecasts were prepared based on income estimates made by the editors for each new book, and forecast comparisons were made on the same basis.

The publisher had two distinct forms of income: that derived from its previously published list, and the estimated new income from soon-to-be-released books. When the income forecast was formulated on the basis of each new book, and as estimated by the acquisitions editors, it was much easier to anticipate the future. The system also led to the design of an incentive system. When an editor's projects exceeded the forecast, he or she earned a bonus.

In situations in which the volume of sales is increasing rapidly, companies tend to allow accounts receivable outstanding balances to move too high. Track the relationship between charge-based sales and accounts receivable average balances to spot negative trends. Also track the average number of days that accounts remain uncollected. If days uncollected increases with sales volume, collection procedures have been relaxed, and this will mean a higher ratio of uncollectible accounts.

Another tendency when revenues are growing is to commit the company to more debt. As receivables grow and remain outstanding, a cash crunch results. And as higher volume means more overhead, borrowing money is an obvious solution. Track the ratio of debt to equity, and suggest that management impose a limit on how much the company will borrow to finance growth.

All of these ideas can come directly from an analysis of cash flow, a crucial element of the budget often overlooked or excluded entirely. The availability of working capital can often make the difference between quality operations and—in an extreme case—a business failure. The bottom-line profits are in some cases secondary to working capital. Cash management problems have forced many minimally financed companies out of business, even while they have reported profits.

Prepare cash flow projections remembering several control points:

1. Modify annual projections to allow for seasonal variances in income volume. Consider not only your own company's volume of sales, but your customers' pattern of payments. Customers' seasonal cash flow will affect your cash receipts directly.
2. Be aware of heavy spending patterns in your organization. Some companies stock up at a particular time of the year, or—due to market factors—must commit funds for promotion in advance of income receipts.
3. Review previous years to identify recurring patterns in working capital. Expect similar surplus or shortage periods in the coming year.
4. Be aware of lag time between booking increases in sales volume and actual receipt of cash. If the company sells on credit, base the projection on established patterns, considering the average number of days that receivables remain uncollected.

Cash flow controls, like income and expense analysis and controls, are natural extentions of the work you must do to develop a sound budget. The research and analysis that create and prove assumptions is of immediate value in creating the budget. But that's only the structure of the system. To make it a working process, follow through and use that information to control the circumstances of operations and to build profits and cash flow.

WORK PROJECT

1. The current budget report reveals an unfavorable variance of 16% in the office supplies account. The percentage has been increasing for the last three months. What steps could improve this condition, and how would you support your arguments?

2. A large unfavorable variance has occurred in your company's gross income forecast. The cause has been identified as lower average production by sales representatives than expected. The original assumption is reasonable, based upon historical levels. What steps should be taken to control the situation?

3. A review of cash flow shows that accounts receivable remain outstanding an average of 54 days. Last year, the average was 43 days. What does this indicate, and what corrective action would you suggest to management?

9
Those Nasty Budget Revisions

The parents of the bride had sent out wedding announcements, but followed up with a second notice. It read, "We regret to inform you that our daughter's wedding, originally planned for July 1, has been delayed until August 5. The groom is unable to attend during the month of July, as he will be working days, evenings, and weekends on budget revisions."

Picture a frazzled manager, sleeves rolled up, unshaven and red-eyed, having gone many days without sleep, buried deep in endless worksheets. All around him, adding machines click and forbidden utterances can be heard under the breath of employees, each buried in their own piles of paperwork. Any personal lives they might have had in the past are now forgotten, at least until they finish the budget revisions.

If you've ever been through a revision, you know all about the pressure and frustration involved. But a revision can and should be an easy and quick process that doesn't take a lot of time and can be completed without the pressure. If you've followed the steps in building assumptions and tracking and identifying variances and their causes, you already have what you need to survive the revision.

FREQUENCY OF REVISIONS

The standard practice in most companies is to prepare a 12-month budget and then to revise after six months. This revision is usually total. It starts from the beginning, with every number developed for six months as though the original budget didn't exist.

Several flaws mar this procedure. First, a soundly structured budget should be used to develop the revised version. You will have learned a great deal from the variances that came up, and should carry over any valid assumptions into the new six-month period. If a budget revision takes the same amount of time as the original budget, question the procedure and suggest a change.

In that situation, why budget for an entire year? Developing 12 months of estimates is pointless if the entire document is going to be replaced in six months. Why not budget for six-month periods instead? Some people will argue that the budget period must correspond to the fiscal year. But why? Since variances "disappear" as soon as the budget is revised, the argument favoring a full year's budgeting does not stand up.

The common argument given to support the full-year budget is that management must be able to estimate its profits for the year. But everyone knows that estimate will change after the second quarter. It makes more sense to estimate profits for six months.

A more practical budgeting approach is to establish a full year's budget and leave it intact, without complete revisions. During the year, specific account budgets may be changed, but only upon determining that basic assumptions are wrong. When variances occur because of control problems, the controls should be put into place. Revising budgets at mid-year is a way of avoiding bringing negative situations under control. The budget is simply increased, and unfavorable trends continue unchecked.

The permanent one-year budget simplifies the process and eliminates the need for the tedious repetition—filling out worksheets, submitting budgets for approval or change, and wasting valuable time. When making predictions, the farther into the future the estimate, the less accurate. That's why six-month revisions are so popular. They assume that the original budget will no longer be valid by then.

Why accept this belief? The original assumptions should retain some validity. As long as they continue to apply, the original budget should remain intact. And if they are invalid, the budget should be changed—even if the problem shows up in the first or second month of the year. Making constant changes can become an administrative nightmare. Obviously, reasonable limits must be set on who can make changes, what is considered a reasonable cause for a change, and the amount of paperwork involved.

The process of changing the budget should be well documented and approved. All control will be lost if the budget can be changed at will and without management approval. Reasons for a change should be questioned and challenged. And take care in changing an account's budget, as any change will, no doubt, affect other accounts.

In one company, an unfavorable variance was discovered in the advertising budget. When the assumption was prepared, a recurring mail campaign to existing customers had been overlooked. Accordingly, a revision was requested. Making the revision required adjusting total expense budgets and estimated net profits. In addition, both the cash projection and income forecast had to be changed:

> The cash flow projection included an estimate of net profits. An increase in advertising expenses changed that figure for the remaining months in the year.
>
> Income had to be changed because overlooking the direct mail campaign also excluded resulting revenues. Forecasts then had to be increased, which also affected cash flow and net profits.

No change can be made in isolation. Virtually any change in the budget requires revising related accounts. If you adopt the full-year budget procedure, you must also put controls into place to ensure that all appropriate accounts are modified.

A variation on this idea is the "rolling" budget. As faulty assumptions are discovered, a change request is made and approved by management. But no changes are made until a six-month revision date. The original budget is prepared for a full year, and revisions are made for the remainder of the 12 months. For example, a calendar year budget runs from January through December. During the first six months, several flaws are discovered in the assumptions, and change requests are made. As of July 1, a revised budget is prepared, incorporating all the approved changes. This budget runs from July 1 through the following June 30, a full twelve months. The process is repeated six months later.

The rolling budget may not always be appropriate. As new markets open up, new yearly strategies and policies are set by management, and the mix of income and expenses changes, a complete budget revision will become necessary.

Even in that case, many of the standing assumptions may remain valid over several periods. For example, a company with a fairly stable employee force can estimate salaries and wages far into the future, given anticipated staff growth and raises. Rent, equipment leases, interest on long-term loans, and other commitments also will remain the same. Expenses like office supplies, printing, and telephone can be controlled substantially, even when the mix of income is changing from one year to the next.

ACCOUNTING FOR VARIANCES

The rolling budget eliminates a common problem. In the typical six-month budget revision, all unfavorable variances simply disappear, and a new, more flexible budget replaces the original. For example, upon discovering that office supplies are running above budget each month, the easy solution is to revise and put a higher allowance into the budget.

That should be allowed *only* if the assumption can be proven wrong. But if the problem is lack of internal control, resulting in a high volume of pilferage and waste, the correct solution is to take control rather than changing the budget.

Whenever a budget is revised, the most important source for information is the previous assumption. Remember that unfavorable variances come up either because that assumption is wrong or because of an internal control problem. Limit revisions to only the first group, and see that control problems are identified and solved.

The revision request procedure should include an analysis of unfavorable variances. Simply making these problems go away by increasing the budget is contrary to the purpose of estimating future income, expenses, and cash flow. Make the process a working tool for creating profits, rather than a time-wasting and mechanical routine.

With a rolling budget, revisions may also come up due to anticipated changes. This can occur even without unfavorable variances. For example, the board of directors approves a plan to expand the company's markets into a new area. This will mean a revision to estimated income, any applicable direct costs, and direct overhead expenses (such as travel, entertainment, telephone, and advertising). This change might also affect fixed overhead accounts such as rent, salaries and wages, and office supplies. An expansion might require a larger support staff (more salary expense), meaning the need for more office or warehouse space (higher rent). Having that larger staff also means allowing more for office supplies. And finally, cash flow projections must also be revised.

A massive change might require an entirely new budget, even with the rolling technique. In that case, carry over any unaffected accounts. For example, long-term loans will continue to affect cash flow and interest expense in the same way, rent on existing facilities will continue under the terms of the existing lease, and salaries for the existing staff will not change.

It makes sense to roll budgets and to make changes immediately upon discovering a flaw. When the budget goes six months before a revision, a discovered problem remains on the books for half the year. The more flexible rolling budget allows for immediate changes.

DOCUMENTING REVISIONS

Whether you revise every six months or use a rolling budget, strive for continuity between periods. Avoid the all too common situation of abandoning a previous budget and starting all over for each revision.

The successes and failures of past budgets offer many lessons. Assumptions are only improved from one period to the next when we carry over the positive and correct the negative. Retain a successful technique for forecasting income in the next period. And modify flaws to make the process more dependable and the resulting comparison more accurate.

Think of the budget flow as a continuous process and not as a solitary job that must be done twice a year:

1. Start with the assumptions. These are the building blocks of the budget and must be the final word. A detailed assumption allows you to determine whether variances are caused by timing differences, faulty estimating, or poor control. This determination also dictates the actions that should be taken.

2. Consider the budget itself (consisting of the income forecast, expense budgets, and cash flow projections) as a permanent goal, but subject to appropriate revisions.
3. Variances are not always problems. They actually present opportunities to correct information. A timing difference will be absorbed, but also suggests how to more accurately time transactions in a future budget. A faulty estimate indicates how to better prepare thorough assumptions. And poor control points the way to increased profits. Reversing an out-of-control trend will save money for the company. This is the essential value of the entire budgeting process.
4. Assumptions can be revised for any of the three causes of variances. Timing differences may recur, requiring rearrangement of future month totals. Wrong assumptions require an immediate change in the budget. And assumptions must also be changed when controls are needed. Some time, perhaps several months, may be required to correct a negative trend, and this curve should be built into the budget.

When any estimate is changed, create a revision flow worksheet, showing not only the change to the one account, but also its effect on the other components of the budget. Figure 9-1 gives an example. Changes for up to 12 months are written in the column for the existing estimate. The next column is for the change. Following this is a summary of the effect on the three sections of the budget: income forecast, net profits, and cash flow.

This worksheet facilitates changes to all sections of your budget workpapers. Keep in a file for later reference the approval of the change and all related worksheets and assumptions. In the monthly report, a simplified summary of status comparing budget and actual and explaining variances, include a footnote the first time the revised budget number is used. Otherwise, keep the report to your budget review committee as simple and summarized as possible.

Place even the smallest change on a worksheet and carry it through to all sections. For example, in one company, the office supplies budget was revised downward by $135 per month because of favorable variance resulting from successfully controlling previously excessive spending levels. The

Figure 9–1

revision worksheet

Account _____

Effective date _____

month	existing estimate	change to:	effect on: income	expenses	cash flow
Total					

change was made in May, and the amount of each month's revision was calculated to absorb the favorable variance existing to that point.

The worksheet was completed as shown in the table.

| | Existing | Change | Effect on: | | |
Month	Estimate	to:	Income	Expenses	Cash Flow
Jan	$2,816				
Feb	2,500				
Mar	3,060				
Apr	2,845				
May	2,790	$2,655		$ (135)	$ 135
Jun	2,996	2,861		(135)	135
Jul	3,000	2,865		(135)	135
Aug	3,000	2,865		(135)	135
Sep	3,000	2,865		(135)	135
Oct	3,000	2,865		(135)	135
Nov	3,000	2,865		(135)	135
Dec	3,000	2,865		(135)	135

The income forecast is not affected as are net profits and cash flow. Changes are made to the summary sheets from this worksheet. The flow of information can be traced all the way from the original budget through any number of revisions to the current summary sheet levels.

Creating and maintaining a valid budget is not a small or simple job. It requires work and constant monitoring over transactions. You must validate coding, investigate sudden timing differences, question assumptions, and revise. Using a rolling budget and initiating changes as they arise eliminates the time required for a complete revision halfway through the year. Of course, the greater the flaws in the original budget, the greater the need for maintenance. But in time, your procedures for developing assumptions will improve, thus cutting down on the time required to manage the entire process.

WORK PROJECT

1. You discover that the unfavorable variance in your income forecast is due to a miscalculation in the original assumption. Some types of income are

booked a full month later than estimated. How would you revise your budget for this problem?

2. Based on the information in the first question, how will the other components of your budget be affected?

3. Management plans to offer a new service to the market, starting in the second half of the year. Following startup costs, this service will generate new revenues and a continuing level of general expenses. Estimates are:

Month	Income	Expenses
Jul	$ -0-	$14,500
Aug	-0-	6,200
Sep	5,900	2,150
Oct	6,800	2,150
Nov	9,400	2,150
Dec	10,300	2,150
Total	$32,400	$29,300

What will be the effect of these changes on each section of the budget?

10

Ten Common Problems and How to Solve Them

It is difficult to get a man to understand something when his job depends upon his not understanding it.

—Upton Sinclair

An executive called his secretary into his office. "You're too organized," he said. "You take it to an extreme, and I'm afraid to even touch the files. I'm afraid to look for anything, and the way you have things arranged, I can't find what I need anyway. We're just going to have to make some changes." After a moment, the secretary asked, "Do you want that in triplicate?"

In budgeting, as with any other business activity, a number of problems recur from year to year in most organizations. Every effort requires balance. The overly organized secretary must learn to balance the need for order, for example; and the preparer of a budget must also be aware that keeping the process valid requires constant modification.

More than ten problems certainly are involved in the budgeting process. The following are the most chronic difficulties, with ideas for solving them.

1. LOSING SIGHT OF REAL OBJECTIVES

Like the overly organized secretary who has made it impossible for the boss to find a file, you might forget *why* you were given the budget assignment. Remember that the process should be an estimate of future income, expenses, and cash flow. It should enable you to pinpoint problems and, thus, devise solutions that will increase profits, cut waste, and help maintain control.

Losing sight of objectives occurs when too much emphasis is placed on completing a complex procedure in a short time, including endless revisions and paperwork. People are so pleased to finally be done with the initial budget they think of it as being completely over. In fact, the job has not even begun.

Control reactions that go into effect during the year can only be practical when they result from discovered variances—when something is wrong with the budget or the actual results (income below expectations, expenses over budget, or cash flow below projected levels).

The vice president of a commercial architectural firm was responsible for the budgeting process. It took her nearly three weeks in December to put the entire income, expense, and cash flow plan down on paper, and she was glad to be done with it. She didn't give it another thought until five months later, in May. It was only then that she realized the budget required monthly review, and she began preparing variance reports. Because she had let it go for so long, she had to deal with several variances. Unfortunately several control opportunities had been lost and she had to take a considerable amount of time to put those controls into effect.

The scope of the project was greater than the vice president had initially thought. If she had taken a couple of hours a month to prepare the report, time and money could have been saved and the budget could have achieved its objectives. She finally realized the job was essential.

To avoid losing sight of the reason you budget, take these steps:

■ Focus every decision toward clear objectives. Think of the budget as a standard, and measure performance against it.

■ Carry through. Begin monthly analysis from the first month of the year. The longer the budget goes without monitoring, the less valid the entire process becomes.

■ Recognize that deferring work on the budget does not save time. Spend a little time each month comparing actual to budget and examining causes, to reduce time in later months.

■ Look in the budget for specific keys to higher profits. Identify ways to either reduce expenses or improve income, and apply controls to make the budgeting process valid.

■ Make a list of control suggestions you have included in your budget, recommendations you've put into monthly reports, and actions management has approved in response. Estimate the savings that have resulted during the year.

2. BUDGETING ABOVE 100% OF LAST YEAR

One of the primary objectives of the budget is to reduce expenses, but a common problem is building lack of control into the budget. For example, last year's expense for dues and subscriptions was 18% over budget, but this year's budget is based on last year's actual.

This common procedure, known as historical-base budgeting, is the easiest way to get through the budget without any real work. Simply take the total spent last year, divide it by 12, and put the result down in each month's column for the coming year. Add a few percentage points for "inflation."

But several things are wrong with this approach. First, last year's expenses were too high, assuming the original budget was reasonable. Accepting this as the base for developing a new budget builds lack of control into the process, which only encourages further excesses.

A different approach is to examine spending policies for each account. Why did the expense exceed budget? An incomplete original assumption should be updated to anticipate all reasonable and necessary expenses. But if the problem is lack of control over spending, some changes should be made.

In one legal firm, each attorney subscribed to his or her own periodical services, often duplicating the same material. No centralized authority approved the spending of money, which made accurate budgeting impossible.

In the previous year, an unfavorable variance resulted. The assumption for the new year included an analysis of the previous year's assumption, and a commentary on the need for better controls. The proposed budget was lower than the previous year's. It was accepted, along with the suggested control procedures, which saved the firm over $4,000 that year.

One caution: It's risky to reduce the budget if you are not authorized to place and enforce controls. For example, the reduced budget might be accepted but your control suggestions largely ignored. In that case, even larger unfavorable variances will occur in that account. For this to be realistic, management has to take the budget seriously—not only the numbers, but the recommendations that go with them.

Avoid the problem of historical-base budgets with these ideas:

- Use historical information as only one assumption source. Also consider possible controls.
- Be especially cautious with budgets in accounts that show unfavorable variances. The solution is not to increase the budget, but rather to devise and enforce practical spending limits.
- Include specific control ideas with suggestions for ways to effect those controls at the beginning of the year.
- Always look for ways to make an expense budget lower than the previous year's, when practicable. Don't make increases automatic.
- Learn from unfavorable variances. The more consistent are variances, the greater the indication of a control problem, a sign that points the way to a solution.

3. GETTING RICH ON PAPER

We can all get rich on paper. Assuming that income will increase significantly each month while expense levels continue to fall will give you a fantastic profit—not in your hand, but on your worksheet. Even when you believe your budget and forecast are reasonable, compare the estimated future results with the most recent actual results. A big difference indicates that the budget needs another look.

In the home office of a securities brokerage firm, the forecast of income for the coming six months was based on faulty assumptions. The office manager based that forecast on a discussion with the vice president of marketing, who estimated that the sales force of 412 people could be doubled within a few months. But not taken into account were several key factors:

It was a seasonal business, and the six months from January through June did not usually include volume as high as the second six months.

There was no allowance for attrition, either among new recruits or the existing sales force.

It was assumed that new production would be booked immediately, when the facts showed that booking took two to three months from the time selling began.

The forecast also assumed that average production would be reported at the same level as that for the existing sales force, which historically was not valid.

Any improvement that goes upward in a straight line is probably unrealistic, especially when estimated results are substantially better than the previous year's. If last year's net income was $200,000, don't expect to earn $400,000 next year. And don't expect to double a sales force in six months, improve the profit margin by 100%, or halve an expense. Positive change can be achieved, but it's more likely to occur gradually.

Follow these steps to avoid developing unrealistic estimates:

- Test all conclusions before they enter the budget. Examine and reexamine all assumptions.
- Compare estimates to the previous year's. Do they seem reasonable in light of actual results from the most recent period? If not, an assumption probably is unrealistic.
- Never base an assumption only on what someone else says, even an expert. Whenever possible, use at least two sources for balance.

4. ACCEPTING ARBITRARY CHANGES

Just as an unrealistic budget will fail, an arbitrary change is valueless. A budget succeeds only if those in positions of authority respect and understand the budgeting process.

This logical philosophy isn't always possible in practice. The people who prepare worksheets and develop assumptions seldom have the final word about the level of income, expense, and cash flow estimates. So no matter how carefully you develop your numbers, and no matter how much sense they make, you can't always prevent someone higher up from changing the budget.

The annual expense budgets in a national overnight delivery service included an increase in aircraft fuel expenses. The assumption was based on planned fuel price increases, and the level of use followed an increase in volume. Even though the fuel consumption estimate was done in line with an acceptable forecast of future revenues, the vice president instructed the manager to lower the expense budget by 10%.

If this happens to you, you can meekly accept the order and make the change or discuss it and try to make your point. If your research is thorough and you believe the budget can be supported, the change should *not* be made. Stick to the facts as you present your arguments. If your disagreement is perceived as a matter of ego, you won't win. Rank will prevail, and even a mistaken change will stand. But a smart executive will back away from a mistake, if opposing facts are presented properly.

Even if you feel completely powerless to change the way someone else thinks and acts, don't assume you can't win a good argument. Follow these guidelines:

- Make a strong case for basing everything on sound assumptions. When a change is ordered, start by asking for a basis that you can document.
- Always work from the strongest possible assumption. If a change is made, present your case and ask for a reversal of the decision.
- Don't allow yourself to be put in the position of having to defend a budget that's been changed arbitrarily. If such a change is made, include a notation on your assumption worksheet explaining who made the change, and use that as part of a later variance explanation.
- Use discretion when arguing with someone who outranks you. Stick to the facts and avoid ego confrontations.

5. BELIEVING THAT BIGGER IS ALWAYS BETTER

Many budget processes are programmed to fail. Just as an executive might arbitrarily reduce an expense budget or increase an income forecast, a common tendency is to think that sales must increase every year.

For example, your company just finished a record year. The dollar amount and percentage of profits had been running at 8% of sales, but last year came in just under 12%. That's an impressive change over the previous four or five years. But what about next year?

It's easy to fall into the trap of thinking you must exceed 12% or results will be negative. So sales must be higher and expenses must be lower.

A photocopier manufacturer lost money last year, even though sales had been higher than in previous periods. That year had seen an expanding marketplace and several new product lines. An analysis of production and marketing revealed that the cost of growth had cut into the margin of profit. Management had to evaluate the situation and make a decision. Some executives thought an investment in expansion would ultimately mean higher profits, but the company would have to accept two or three years of loss. But the president was concerned about growing too rapidly and wanted to emphasize controlled growth with customer service placed above volume.

It's often necessary to cut back on volume to improve net profits, or even to purposely not grow in order to preserve quality. When volume is too costly to continue and won't ultimately improve quality or profits, growth for its own sake makes no sense. Don't think in terms of unrelenting improvement. Not every expense account will move downward each year, and gross revenues won't always increase. Real progress occurs in a series of small successes and failures, which must be accepted as a part of the process of growth.

Be realistic when preparing the budget. Set a goal to reduce expenses and increase revenue when possible, but only within the boundaries of realistic estimates. Follow these steps:

■ Don't become alarmed if your budget shows a lower profit than the previous year. Accept that as part of the ebb and flow of running an organization.

■ Recognize that long-term growth might include one or more years of loss that represent the investment a business makes to expand.

■ Support lower income forecasts or higher expense budgets with solid research and assumptions.

■ Expect resistance to any budget that doesn't exceed the previous year's, and always point to the assumptions that support your estimates.

6. RESPONDING TO "EXPLANATION PRESSURE"

Realism also helps explain the inevitable variances that arise. A variance, small or large, is not necessarily a sign the budget is wrong. Rather, it's a signal that you need to exert controls over income or expenses. A problem can be solved only when you know what it is.

Still, if management places too much emphasis on "accuracy" in the budget, it's easy to begin to dread any significant variance. This dread may lead to explanations that hide the truth rather than lead management to corrective action.

That was the problem at a large answering service. So much emphasis was placed on accuracy in budgets that, when variances did appear, the chief accountant wanted to know who was responsible. This is a management attitude problem: looking for people problems when processes are to blame. The effort to come up with an acceptable explanation diverted attention from discovering and solving the real problem. No one was willing to admit that an assumption was incomplete, that too much money was being spent, or that income simply wasn't being earned at the forecast rate.

In such a situation the budget is being used only as a tool for blame. No problems are solved, because they're not being reported. Follow these steps to solve this problem:

- Always go back to the assumption when writing a variance explanation, and base it on a comparison.
- Identify real problems—weak or incomplete assumptions, excessive spending, or lack of control. Recommend solutions rather than placing blame.
- Don't respond to real or perceived personal assignment of responsibility. Recognize the budgeting process as one that monitors processes only.
- Think of budgeting as a guideline, not an infallible indicator of the future. No one can do better than an estimate, and variances will arise.
- Emphasize immediate solutions, going beyond mere identification of causes for variances.

7. DEPENDING HEAVILY ON STATISTICS

Explanation pressure is a common failing of the budgeting process, but a closely related problem is depending too heavily on numbers, which results in manipulating the facts.

Typical abuse of statistics includes the drafting of explanations that don't identify causes but rather attempt to indicate a trend (often, where a trend doesn't even exist).

Consider this example: "The 11% unfavorable variance is an improvement over last year, when the same expense was 17% over budget." This bit of historical information tells nothing of the cause for the variance. If anything, it shows the results of increasing a budget for an account that's out of control and has been since last year.

Another use of statistics that gives the reader no real value could read: "Of 17 general expense accounts, only five showed unfavorable variances. So 71% of all accounts are under budget, compared with 64% last quarter." Missing from this is any constructive indication of problems or where they exist. The number of accounts in variance is of no real interest or meaning.

This is a two-sided problem. First is that of the preparer who attempts to locate trends, to look for a sign that things are improving rather than dealing with the real issue of control. Second is the acceptance of the statistical statement or a perceived trend by management. In many companies the interesting but useless statement is taken for useful information. Then, management itself accepts the illusion that, somehow, a positive trend is under way.

Rise above the mundane packaging of budget reports that include useless statistics. Identify problems and offer solutions. Indicate a course of action. Make your variance report valid and essential to management. Management then will notice your report and respond to it.

One consulting firm experienced unfavorable variances in several accounts every year, but accepted the budget preparer's view that the situation was improving. In the variance report, this year's problems were constantly compared to the previous year's, and statistical "trends" showed a decline in the rate of variance. This didn't solve the problem though, because the budget for problem accounts was being increased each year. A better way to deal with the problem would be to develop a reasonable budget and then control the level of expense.

Approach budgeting from a realistic perspective and use statistics only to explain a clear trend. Follow these guidelines:

- Don't try to excuse excessive spending or disappointing revenues by referring to a previous period. Confront the problems that exist *this* year.
- Don't request an increase in this year's budget because last year's went over. If there's a control problem, work on solutions rather than escalating a bad situation.
- Avoid using weak assumptions. These lead to an inability to identify or

explain problems. This inability might tempt you to turn to the statistical alternative in search of an explanation that at least sounds reasonable.

8. KEEPING INACCURATE BUDGETS IN EFFECT

One of the ironies of budgeting in some companies is that discovered problems are not only left unsolved but are allowed to continue.

As an example, an office furniture rental firm had underestimated advertising expenses. Only a couple of months into the year, everyone on the review committee realized the error, which would cause variances in that account all year. Yet they did not change the budget.

Small discrepancies should not effect a major budget revision. Correcting for every discovered problem would make budgeting take even more time than it does now. You'd be involved in endless monthly revisions. But when a major account is grossly wrong, an immediate change should be offered, accepted, and enacted.

Faults may also be carried forward to future years. Will you learn from past mistakes or repeat them? Certain accounts are always difficult to control by their nature, depending upon the industry, internal reporting and spending policies, and the way in which budgets are prepared.

Take these steps to keep your company from having to live with its mistakes:

- Suggest immediate changes in response to a major error.
- Develop a system for changing budgets within the period rather than having to wait until the next revision date. Build in simplicity and complete documentation, and make sensible change as practicable as possible.
- Start each year's budgeting process with a review of the previous year. List the problems that were discovered throughout the year and make certain they're not repeated.
- If you find errors carried forward from one month to another, point them out in subsequent variance reports. Show management that problems will not go away by themselves, but must be solved. No control is possible when working from a faulty base.

9. ACCEPTING RESPONSIBILITY WITHOUT AUTHORITY

A person who prepares budgets might believe he or she has no voice in the decisionmaking process. Thus, problems like inaccurate assumptions are never fixed. As the year progresses, the process itself becomes a joke in the company. Demoralization occurs if you let yourself be placed in the most difficult position of all—having responsibility without the corresponding authority.

In one insurance company, the manager of the accounting department had to prepare the monthly budget variance report. But because budgets were prepared in different departments, he was not authorized to make changes in the budget, or even to recommend actions that he found obvious. His one past suggestion regarding the marketing department's need for internal controls created a real power problem with bad consequences.

That manager allowed himself to be placed in an impossible situation. He had to explain problems but lacked the authority to even offer a solution. That lack of communication and poor organizational structure is backward thinking by management. Realistically, if top management is unaware of a problem, or if it allows political motivation behind what should be a progressive form of communication, there's simply no improvement to make. But if your top management is more progressive than that, take the initiative to suggest a change.

Follow these steps to improve your lack of authority:

- When you do have responsibility but not authority, point out the problem to those in a position to make changes.
- Carefully monitor the tone of your recommendations. Present ideas and point to the absolute facts, but allow management to come to its own conclusions and initiate action.
- Ask for authority. It's better to try to take on a challenge than to live with passive budgeting and suffer its consequences.
- If your solution will involve another department, visit with the manager before the budget review meeting. Disclose what you've concluded and discuss the proposed solution in advance, asking for an opinion or a reaction. This prevents embarrassing surprises at the meeting and perceptions of political motives behind even your best intentions.
- Keep all lines of communication open—between departments, with your immediate supervisor, and with everyone in positions of authority and responsibility. Attempt to develop joint solutions rather than playing the role of adversary.

10. FAILING TO RECOMMEND

If you've been burned because well-intended budget recommendations were taken as invasions into the territory of another department, that's a sign of poor communication. It also may discourage you from making constructive statements.

In response to past confrontations, and because many people fear taking the initiative, budget reports seldom include recommendations. They're passive. For example, you might find that income is being reported far below anticipated levels, and identify the problem as one of lagging production. You want to make the recommendation to impose specific monitoring and quotas at the sales office level, but you fear alienating executives in a powerful and influential marketing department. So you restrict your comments to an identification of causes for the unfavorable variance.

That's what occurred in one telephone sales company. The forecast of income was based on an individually prepared production schedule, including quotas. The manager preparing the budget observed that a large portion of the sales force was falling behind the same levels in the previous year. But the explanation in the variance report merely commented on the causes of the problem.

Not surprisingly, management did not act—because it hadn't been given a recommendation. Don't expect anyone to come up with action ideas if you simply point to the problem. Make a specific recommendation for immediate action in response to any variance. That really puts the budget to use.

Follow these guidelines to avoid this most common of problems:

- Don't write your explanations the way they've always been written in the past. Go beyond identifying problems to offer answers.
- If your solutions will include imposing changes in another department, communicate with the manager before the meeting, just as you would do to solve the problem of having responsibility without authority.
- Present solutions jointly with an outside manager. Communicate the solution as one that you both agree upon, and avoid disputes and uncertainty.
- Assume that management depends on your analytical talents and expertise in interpreting the budget, and develop solutions accordingly. Think of yourself as the expert on the budget you've prepared and researched, and be willing to offer your ideas.

▪ Encourage specific deadlines for action, so that management can respond just as specifically.

▪ If your recommendations are not acted upon, remind management. Point out in the following month's report that the problem is still there, and make the recommendation again.

*　*　*

For the amount of effort that goes into preparation of a budget, it should have a specific, recognizable result. Unfortunately, managers of many companies wait for a crisis before acting.

Help your company avert a crisis by showing how to take action today. Avoid out-of-control situations with planning, by keeping an eye on the future, and by respecting the real meaning behind a trend. The goal of your budget is not accuracy per se but rather the setting of standards. An income or expense account that happens to closely match your budget indicates strength and accuracy in your assumptions. The absence of a problem is a worthy accomplishment.

Effort must be expended, though, in addressing the issues raised when variances are discovered. In too many organizations, a large variance is cited as proof of the mistaken belief that the future cannot be controlled. If that's true, what is the function of management? You're the supervisor of your own budget, and that job does, indeed, require a "super vision" of the future. It also demands that problems must be identified and confronted at once, through the action of the right solution. By knowing the common problems that arise in the budgeting process, you can develop a sense of what to avoid and how to make the entire process valid and profitable.

WORK PROJECT

1. Last year's sales were significantly higher than in any previous year. You're instructed to prepare a forecast for the new year on the assumption that sales will continue to increase. You believe this assumption is wrong. How will you argue your case?

2. A lot of research went into developing assumptions for travel expenses. You've identified every known expense in the coming six months and

eliminated all general estimates from the budget. Your concern is that no allowance has been included for unknown travel. Even so, your boss wants to cut $500 a month from the estimate. What will you do?

3. The current budget was prepared before management decided to open a second office and hire several new employees. Now, salary, payroll tax, and rent accounts are entirely out of date. What recommendations will you make in the budget review meeting?

11

Budgets and Your Career

Management by objective works if you know the objectives.
Ninety percent of the time you don't.

—Peter F. Drucker

When Bob finished giving his budget report, he went to visit with his friend, Andy. "I've noticed that the president sometimes clips his nails during meetings," Bob said. "Don't you think that's rude?" Andy explained, "Oh, he only does that when he's bored by what he's hearing. Why? Was he clipping while you spoke?" "Yeah," Bob mumbled, turning white. "He drew blood."

It's not easy to make budget reports interesting. Even the best information, if presented wrong, can do more harm than good. Being a skilled preparer of budgets exceeds being able to compile and analyze information. You also have to be able to communicate it well.

That communication must contain practical solutions to identified problems. It must be presented with a sensitivity to the company's political climate. And it must hold the interest of others. So the report must be brief and simple, yet so useful that it cannot be ignored.

UNDERSTANDING OBJECTIVES

Budget reporting is a communication skill. Whether you convey your conclusions in person or through a memo or report, you must be able to address the issues that management considers valid. It's not enough to base conclusions on what you want. You must also understand how management views the company's priorities.

For example, the marketing director of a financial services corporation reported that income was above the forecast. He commented to the budget review committee that revenues for the year could be expanded far beyond the original forecast. The president asked, "If income is higher than we estimated, why are we losing money?"

The objective of that year's budget had been stated clearly. Management wanted to cut expenses and achieve higher profits. The cost of expanding gross income was not acceptable, and the emphasis in the budget should have been to pursue that objective. The marketing director, who understood only the sales end of the issue, didn't see the connection.

Budgets succeed when they are prepared, controlled, and operated within the context of a larger company objective. Unfortunately, some companies don't make an effort to publish an objective, and a lot of employees don't really know what an objective is or should be. In one progressive firm, the president gathered together all of the executives and managers and gave them an assignment: Write down the business this organization is in. The 17 people in the meeting came up with 17 different answers. The president responded by spending several days drafting a four-sentence objective.

Setting objectives might seem far removed from the budgeting process. But it isn't. The budget, like the rest of the company's work, should be a coordinated and well-communicated effort. In too many organizations, individual managers and supervisors develop their own objectives and impose them on the people in their department. In that environment, the company never operates toward a single objective. But successful and well-run companies have one thing in common: Everyone does understand the business they're in and knows its objective.

SURVIVING THE PRESSURE

When everyone knows the objective, the chance for healthy two-way communication improves. You can have a different point of view than that held by another department head, but still work toward the same end result. And that will be reflected in the attitude everyone has toward the budget.

We can easily become distracted and lose a valid point of view because of poor communication, conflicting motives, and personal objectives that are different from the company's. For example, the manager of one department might take a suggestion for tightening up on expenses as a personal threat. In some cases, no matter how carefully you phrase a recommendation, someone will think you're out of line.

The solution? Always stay within the framework of the company's objective, and always base your suggestions on approved assumptions.

Budgets should be the means for defining objectives in financial terms. That might take a lot of analysis, but by keeping a perspective on the purpose of budgeting, you can survive the process and stay in control. Remember that the budget is not the objective, but only a way to reach it.

One accounting manager worked for several weeks to prepare a final budget. So much work had gone into documenting assumptions, completing analysis, and supporting every part of the budget, that he failed to put it into action as a control process. He lost his perspective.

In another case, the manager of the marketing department spent as little time as possible on the budget, preferring to spend her time more creatively. When it came time to explain variances, she had no base to refer to.

Both of these examples represent extremes in attitude that can and should be balanced. The first is an obsession with paperwork to the point that the budget becomes more significant than operating the company. The second is complete disdain for the budgeting process. When it comes time to do a variance report, the people at neither extreme are prepared to handle what comes up, or to address the real, significant issues at hand.

Your attitude toward your budgeting responsibilities says a lot about your attitude toward your job. Those who succeed know what management needs and wants, and develop ways to build toward that. If you are overly concerned with paperwork, that attitude will come through in all of your communications. And if you don't want to spend more than an hour or two doing your budget, you won't be able to solve problems that come up during the year.

Many managers are put under severe pressure in the budgeting process. Respond with balance. Spend enough time to identify the elements of control over income, expenses, and cash flow. Then refer to the standards set in your budget for evaluation. That's what a variance report really is, a summary of how actual performance measures up to the assumed acceptable level of performance.

Management cannot expect monthly reports that include no big variances. They are inevitable. The test of your performance is not the accuracy of your budget, but the way you handle the problems that come along. In one insurance company, a manager commented that his previous year's budget was very successful because only a few variances occurred over the whole year. But a careful look showed that expenses had risen in most major accounts, while business hadn't increased much.

In another department, a manager had experienced several significant variances. But the final results for the year came in with lower overall expenses for the department, even though responsibilities had increased. From the top, that was the more successful department.

The difference was in the approach to the process. It is easy to prepare ahead by increasing budgets in problem accounts, which will ensure no serious variances. But that's not control. It's distortion rather than planning.

Control. That's what the budget is for. The manager who had variances devised ways to cut expenses because he saw variances as problems waiting to be solved. And it paid off. The department's expenses were cut for the year.

In the final analysis, management judges employees by results. Lower expenses with higher levels of performance is success. No one is going to remember that you got through the year without going over budget, especially if your department's expenses rose at the same time. "Performance" can be measured as improvement in quality of service or products; as more quantity of production with the same staff; or as progress in the development of systems or controls.

YOUR PERSONAL ATTITUDE

Your standing in your company will be judged on the basis of several factors, including the following:

1. Communication skills. How well do you convey information? Are

you able to quickly get to the issue itself? Can you make a complex issue simple? And are you prepared for meetings?

2. Confidence. It might be said that employees will be remembered in two ways: by the degree of confidence or by the degree of lack of confidence. Always prepare well before communicating information. Anticipate questions; answer them before they're asked. State what you have to say in as few words as possible, but be prepared to defend everything you say with absolute and indisputable facts. You won't have to argue if you have proof.

3. Solutions. If you want to advance in your company, do not limit yourself to the disclosure of problems. Disclosure should only be the premise for the more important presentation of a solution. Most employees fail to assume responsibility for solving, but are content to merely report. Rise above that attitude, and you'll be recognized as someone worth keeping, to be given a greater level of responsibility, and to turn to for answers.

These points—communication, confidence, and solutions—apply to every phase of your job. Budget reporting is a forum that presents opportunities. That process is deeply dependent upon all three attributes. While it may not be the primary function of your job, it is an excellent chance to show what you can do.

Developing these skills in the preparation, reporting, and solving of budget problems will also improve your skills in every other phase of your job. By knowing company objectives, offering solutions rather than problems, and communicating clearly and with confidence, you will become highly skilled in everything else you do.

FORECASTING YOUR OWN FUTURE

Begin thinking about your own career in terms of a forecast. You estimate income by making assumptions about the market, a sales force, competition, and several other related factors. Use the same tactic in planning your own career.

Do you live your ambitions? Most people, even those with specific ideas about where they're going, don't make the difference for themselves of living that ambition. The steps to follow in translating ambitions into tangible progress are a lot like those taken to build an income forecast:

- Be aware of your actions and how they add to or take away from where you want to go.
- Develop assumptions about how you plan to advance in your company, based on observation and experience.
- Evaluate your plan often, and decide what changes you need to make.
- Accept change in yourself. Just as time and events modify an income forecast, your career goals will change.
- Monitor results. Take pride in advances you earn and get, but also learn from setbacks. These are not failures; use them to avoid future mistakes and to improve your career forecasting abilities.
- Take pride in your communications. Don't put anything in writing or make any statements that you haven't researched completely. Anticipate answers to questions before they're asked. That will make the greatest impression of all.

Budgets are not the most important service you provide to your company, nor are they your career lifeline. But looking into the future and estimating it is a habit that helps you in many ways. Properly structured, a budget is the alarm that goes off when a problem comes up. You can answer with solutions, so that valuable and needed information grows out of the process itself. That works, whether in a budget or as part of your career path.

Keep your perspectives on your career, just as you must for paperwork backing up your budget. Stay in control, think like a leader, and raise problems only to show how they can be solved. That's the way to make a career grow. The good budget may be rife with variances before the year is done, but still succeed in terms of the solutions developed in response to it. Your career works that way, too. Advancing in your company will not be a smooth or easy path without twists and turns. Pitfalls hide along the way. And success without those problems would hardly be rewarding. Growth comes not by avoiding difficulty, but by facing and overcoming it.

WORK PROJECT

1. You're preparing for a presentation to the budget review committee and find that your department has a large variance in its dues and subscriptions expense account. What should be the steps in your preparation?

2. The budget report in your company is sent out to executives at the

end of each month. You rarely hear any response. What steps might you take to improve internal communication?

3. An employee in your department asks you to sign for a new typewriter. The reason given for the request is, "Another employee got one, so why can't I have one, too?" What advice should you give to this employee?

Appendix A
Work Project Answers

CHAPTER 1

1. Budgets based on the previous year create several problems. First, no room exists for correction of negative trends. If last year's budget was too high, it contains a built-in tendency for overspending. Second, if you must later explain why variances occur, you will have a poor assumption to compare to. Third, the budget is not based on sound assumptions such as an increased number of employees, inflation in prices, or other specific and logical points. A 10% increase would be appropriate only when based on a specific estimate, such as price increases, growth in the number of employees, or expansion of facilities.

2. Instruct employees to base their estimates on known or assumed changes. For example, if the company has just opened an overseas office, expect long-distance calls to increase. If a pending rate change will affect you, take it into account. And if you reacted to a previous unfavorable variance by installing controls, they will reduce future expenses.

3. Make suggestions to other departments with tact and you will get results. For example, point out that with fewer divisions (or salespeople), the requirement will be lower. Then ask for a revised budget. This argument can work in reverse, too. If the manager submitted numbers similar to the previous year's, but you know the company is expanding, the amounts may be insufficient.

CHAPTER 2

1. Always start with the assumptions that went into the original budget. How was the printing budget developed? Compare the levels of assumptions with actual expenses this year. If the budget is not in line with the necessary spending level, that is your first possibility. If the assumption is sound, look for excessive spending. Can costs be

cut in the immediate future? It may be that an unusually high number of forms or stationery was ordered to get a price break. Or you may need to compare prices between different printers. You may also be able to get a price break by combining several orders.

2. Examine the forecast assumption carefully. If many of the existing salespeople are new recruits, was it realistic to expect them to match the volume of more experienced people? With a higher number of inexperienced salespeople, you must also expect lower volume for several months. Another possibility is the failure to create and enforce specific volume goals for individuals. You may suggest a thorough analysis of volume for those with the company two years or more, compared with those with two years or less experience. Then recommend either a more realistic forecast and revision, or development of goals and incentives to meet the forecast.

3. This most common problem can be overcome if you can prove to management that it will save money by investing in a new employee. If you argue that you have too much work and not enough staff, do not expect a favorable response. Show how and why you must hire a new employee. For example, you can demonstrate that you'll be able to eliminate overtime, or provide a level of service that management expects but cannot achieve with a limited staff, or save money by exercising control over expenses that isn't possible now.

CHAPTER 3

1. Where there is no history, you must depend on similar situations and the state of the market and competition. You could analyze the volume experience in products of a similar price and nature sold to the same market. Also consider whether the potential market is stronger or weaker than it was for the other product. Other factors include customers for other lines of business and the amount of competition. For example, if current purchasers of other products might respond well to what you're offering now, they might be a fairly dependable source for sales. If your product is similar to several others on the market today, how does it's price compare? As many

factors as possible should be considered when you are on new ground.

2. Forecasts based on recruitment should be made net of attrition. Study the past record for new recruits. What was average first-year production? How many left during the first 12 months? And what were the costs associated with recruiting and training new people? Also be sure that income generated by projected new recruits is timed realistically. It won't necessarily show up for several months.

3. Examine the forecast growth assumptions to make certain that allowances are included for schedule delays or setbacks. The plan may be overly aggressive, meaning you haven't figured on competition, loss of past revenue sources, or delays in putting a marketing plan into effect. The point: to avoid committing to permanent overhead if growth involves substantial risks. A complete analysis of both income and affected overhead accounts should be conducted before the plan is approved.

CHAPTER 4

1. When an account has been poorly controlled (from a coding point of view) your assumptions cannot be built from historical information. Begin instead with an analysis of the account, identifying what should and shouldn't be there. Then build assumptions using the four elements (information sources, growth, timing, and controls) with special emphasis on controls. As part of your assumption base, show the need for improved coding procedures and possibly a system for requisitioning or centralizing the purchase and distribution of supplies.

2. You will need the following information:
   a. Historical levels of expense, preferably broken down by department or individual.
   b. Forecasts of next year's sales volume, especially if expansion is planned.
   c. Marketing plans for future development of new markets, customers, geographic expansion, and other significant factors.
   d. Controls on individual authorization for travel and entertain-

ment expense (if these do not exist, suggest them as part of your assumption).

3. When asking your company to spend money, always look at the project from a management point of view. How will the project produce profits or improve customer service? Emphasize the features of your proposal that meet *those* objectives. Then support your proposal with information based in fact. How will improved access make your department more efficient or profitable? Will you be able to eliminate overtime or replace a system that's expensive to maintain? Gather financial information and estimate profits or reduced costs. Whenever possible, also estimate the time required to break even or begin making a profit.

CHAPTER 5

1. Current ratio is computed by dividing current assets by current liabilities. Ratios for the four months are as follows:

January	2.13 to 1
February	2.02 to 1
March	1.96 to 1
April	1.95 to 1

The direction of the trend appears to be negative (although, as a general rule, you would need to review a longer period to establish this trend dependably). Possible contributing factors may include: lack of control over average accounts receivable balances left uncollected, poor inventory management, an excessive level of current expense purchases, a too-high level of current notes payable and related debt service, or excessive commitments of cash for the purchase of fixed assets or funding of expansion programs.

2. Include in your assumption base all information from the following sources: current conditions (such as the existing level of note payments), known plans for acquisitions and disposals of capital assets, estimates of accounts receivable and payable activity during the year, and forecasts/budgets of income and expenses. Also include information on planned new loans or asset acquisitions, or debt retirement. Break assumptions down into monthly projections on an

individual basis, and then combine the results of your assumption worksheets into a comprehensive and well-documented report.

3. Negative cash flow can be caused by a combination of factors, including: excessive planned investment in an expansion program, acquisition of capital assets (requiring cash payments or debt service), too rapid a schedule for the reduction or retirement of existing debt, lax controls over operating expense levels, poor control of inventory (resulting in pilferage, damage, or stock becoming obsolete), or a high purchase level caused by volume buying to get discounts (for inventory or general expenses).

CHAPTER 6

1. Your assumptions can be based on one or more of the following:
   last year's actual travel expenses
   the current period's marketing plan
   expense controls in place (for discount fares and combined trips, for example)
   executive travel planned and approved for the coming period

2. Each of the components of the budget must be broken down and fully explained on detail sheets. The budget worksheet should summarize the financial results of those assumptions:

Month	(1)	(2)	(3)	Total
Jan	$ 850	$ 0	$ 475	$ 1,325
Feb	850	0	475	1,325
Mar	850	1,200	475	2,525
Apr	850	0	475	1,325
May	850	0	475	1,325
Jun	850	0	475	1,325
Jul	850	0	499	1,349
Aug	850	1,200	499	2,549
Sep	850	0	499	1,349
Oct	850	0	499	1,349
Nov	850	0	499	1,349
Dec	850	0	499	1,349
Total	10,200	2,400	5,844	18,444

3. The report should be broken down by assumption, with totals for each month and a grand total for the entire year:

(1) A recurring expense for (description) is estimated to begin at $550 and grow by 3% per month (see explanation on detailed analysis, ref. III-16).

(2) Payments in March, June, and October will be made for (explanation), of $4,000 each.

(3) The expense of (description) is estimated to run $385 for the first four months, to increase by 10% beginning in the fifth month, and another 5% beginning in the ninth month (see detailed analysis, ref. III-18).

Summary:

Month	(1)	(2)	(3)	Total
Jan	550		385	935
Feb	567		385	952
Mar	583	4,000	385	4,968
Apr	601		385	986
May	619		424	1,043
Jun	638	4,000	424	5,062
Jul	657		424	1,081
Aug	676		424	1,100
Sep	697		445	1,142
Oct	718	4,000	445	5,163
Nov	739		445	1,184
Dec	761		445	1,206
Total	7,806	12,000	5,016	24,822

CHAPTER 7

1. In the case of income, a higher actual result is favorable. For expenses, higher actual results are unfavorable. So the variances are:

Account	Actual	Budget	Variance	%
Income	$886,703	$846,750	$39,953	4.7
Travel	42,855	38,300	(4,555)	(11.9)
Entertainment	9,010	10,000	990	9.9
Office supplies	10,861	10,400	(461)	(4.4)

2. The income variance is not significant. Although it far exceeds the $500 level, it represents only 4.7% of the budget. The office supplies variance is short of the standard on the dollar and percentage tests.

3. This is clearly a timing difference rather than a problem. The explanation could read, "The favorable variance is caused by an assumption that the entire expense would be incurred and paid during the month of May. We were billed only $6,200. The remaining balance is expected during June, and the favorable condition will be absorbed."

CHAPTER 8

1. The fact that the unfavorable variance is growing establishes a serious problem. If your company does not have a formalized procedure for ordering and approving supply purchases, it should be considered now. Also suggest locking up supplies to avoid pilferage and establishing a requisitioning system for internal supply requests. This formality is effective in discouraging misuse. Support your arguments for tighter controls by pointing out that the budget was based upon reasonable assumptions. The unfavorable variance is further proof that better controls are essential.
2. Recommend that the sales and marketing department analyze production on an individual basis, with the intention of imposing individual production goals. It might also be necessary to examine the effectiveness of regional sales management in comparison to previous periods. Reduce the problem to the individual level to reach a reasonable forecast assumption.
3. An increase in the average days that accounts are outstanding is a sign that collection procedures have been relaxed. This is likely to occur during periods of volume expansion, but invariably leads to higher levels of bad debt. Suggest a review of collection procedures and an emphasis on the importance of reducing the outstanding accounts within fewer days. Also suggest tracking this trend regularly to ensure its success.

CHAPTER 9

1. Upon discovering a flaw in your assumption, you have two choices: Either note the flaw and comment upon it every month, or recom-

mend a revision. Income should be restated on a more accurate basis, and this discovered problem should be sufficient reason to make a change.

2. On the summary sheets, net profits must be adjusted to reflect the change to each month. It is also possible that estimated total profits for the year will be lower due to a delay in booking income. Cash flow projections will also be affected by this change. Less cash will be available than originally estimated.

3. This change will affect every component of the budget. A worksheet should be prepared summarizing the revision flow, and including working papers for revised assumptions. Since this revision involves both income and expenses, include the net change in the "change to" column, and then show the effect on each section of the budget:

Month	Existing estimate	Change to:	Effect on: Income	Effect on: Expenses	Effect on: Cash flow
Jul	$ 0	$(14,500)	$ 0	$14,500	$(14,500)
Aug	0	(6,200)	0	6,200	(6,200)
Sep	0	3,750	5,900	2,150	3,750
Oct	0	4,650	6,800	2,150	4,650
Nov	0	7,250	9,400	2,150	7,250
Dec	0	8,150	10,300	2,150	8,150
Total	$ 0	$ 3,100	$32,400	$29,300	$ 3,100

CHAPTER 10

1. This is a typical problem in budget preparation. An unusually positive trend, even if unrealistic, is expected to continue. Before arguing for a more realistic approach, develop fully researched assumptions and make the forecast as realistic as possible. Then present your arguments to your supervisor, pointing to the assumption and not just a belief that the unusually high level of revenues won't be repeated.

2. Arbitrary change builds failure into the budget. If you know actual expenses will be greater than a changed estimate, the process isn't being used correctly. Show your boss how you developed the budget, make the point that it's already as lean as possible, and ask for a

reversal of the decision to reduce it. If that's refused, document the source of the change, and refer to it in variance reports. It isn't necessary to blame your boss for an arbitrary decision; use discretion. For example, you might refer to the original assumptions, then state that "the budget was further reduced in an effort to reduce the level of expense."

3. Unknown events that make budgets obsolete are cause for a mid-year revision. Prepare new assumptions and suggest a change in the budget. Emphasize the need for realistic controls from one month to another. If your ideas are not accepted, include a reminder in your explanation each month that the budget is no longer applicable in the changed environment, and repeat recommendations for a new budget.

CHAPTER 11

1. Always go into meetings with all of your facts in hand. Thorough research leads to clear communication, identification of priorities, and clarity in your presentation. Be prepared to explain why the variance occurred, and devise at least two possible solutions that you're ready to put into action.

2. Remote communication is the most difficult and the least likely to lead to action. Encourage your supervisor to suggest a better forum, such as a brief monthly meeting among department heads. Also consider following up written reports with a request for responses to your ideas for solutions.

3. This is a typical request made from the point of view of a problem rather than a solution. Advise the employee to take a different approach whenever making requests. The request should always include clear proof that a positive response will save money, make procedures more efficient, or in some other way improve conditions. Rather than presenting problems to supervisors, suggest to the employee that more can be expected by suggesting solutions.

Appendix B
The Complete Budget

Following is a sample complete budget for a fictitious corporation called On-Line Consultants, Inc. It is a greatly simplified example but includes the income forecast, expense budget, and cash flow projections. In addition to a cover memo and summary sheets it includes documentation of all assumptions. Excluded are the detailed worksheets that would be necessary to support and develop these results.

A six-month example is given on the premise that the budget will be completely revised after that period.

This corporation provides services to a variety of clients under consulting agreements. On-Line reviews a company's volume and nature of transactions, prepares workflow summaries, and recommends methods for achieving full automation. Consulting agreements continue during the conversion period and beyond. The firm may develop software or recommend existing software programs and packages. It also researches and recommends hardware purchases.

The examples can be applied to departmental or to company budgets, even on a larger, more complex scale. The budget shows different methods of building assumptions and cross-references between related documents.

COVER MEMO

On-Line Consultants, Inc.

Memo on Forecast and Budget

Enclosed is the forecast, budget, and cash projection for the next six months. After-tax profits are estimated at 19.8% of gross revenues, which compares to profits over the last three six-month periods of 17.7%, 20.4%, and 19.0%, respectively.

The corporation is continuing to pay $8,000 per month toward purchase of the building it occupies, under a lease-purchase agreement with the present owner. At the end of the forecast period, the total deposited toward the down-payment will be $88,000.

The complete forecast, budget, and projection is summarized on the first sheets and supported with explanations of all assumptions. Detailed work-sheets are available upon request.

On-Line Consultants, Inc.
Forecast and Budget

Description	Ref.	Jan	Feb	Mar
Gross Sales	A	$45,600	$49,000	$48,040
Salaries and wages	B	$21,250	$21,250	$24,370
Payroll taxes	C	2,401	2,401	2,754
Employee benefits	D	1,162	1,162	1,328
Travel, entertainment	E	768	5,168	993
Advertising	F	318	318	318
Printing	G	24	24	60
Office supplies	H	419	419	479
Interest expense	I	153	151	150
Rent	J	1,150	1,150	1,150
Postage and delivery	K	316	316	316
Dues, subscriptions	L	-	35	-
Equipment leases	M	479	479	479
Telephone, utilities	N	1,120	1,120	1,120
Repairs, maintenance	O	1,235	-	216
Insurance	P	351	351	359
Legal, professional	Q	800	800	5,000
Depreciation	R	621	621	621
Miscellaneous	S	75	75	75
Total expenses		$32,642	$35,840	$39,788
Operating profit		$12,958	$13,160	$ 8,252
Provision for taxes	T	1,944	1,974	1,238
Net profit		$11,014	$11,186	$ 7,014

On-Line Consultants, Inc.
Forecast and Budget

Description	Apr	May	Jun	Total
Gross Sales	$49,800	$49,800	$51,910	$294,150
Salaries and wages	$24,370	$27,490	$27,700	$146,430
Payroll taxes	2,754	3,106	3,130	16,546
Employee benefits	1,328	1,494	1,510	7,984
Travel, entertainment	993	1,218	1,218	10,358
Advertising	331	331	331	1,947
Printing	24	60	24	216
Office Supplies	479	539	539	2,874
Interest expense	306	298	290	1,348
Rent	1,150	1,150	1,150	6,900
Postage and delivery	316	316	316	1,896
Dues, subscriptions	42	268	-	345
Equipment leases	479	479	479	2,874
Telephone, utilities	1,096	1,096	1,096	6,648
Repairs, maintenance	-	-	-	1,451
Insurance	359	366	367	2,153
Legal, professional	800	800	800	9,000
Depreciation	621	621	621	3,726
Miscellaneous	75	75	75	450
Total expenses	$35,523	$39,707	$39,646	$223,146
Operating profit	$14,277	$10,093	$12,264	$ 71,004
Provision for taxes	2,142	2,388	3,064	12,750
Net profit	$12,135	$ 7,705	$ 9,200	$ 58,254

On-Line Consultants, Inc.
Cash Flow Projection

Description	Ref.	Jan	Feb	Mar
Cash, beginning balance		$ 4,160	$ 5,972	$8,009
Plus:				
Net profit		$11,014	$11,186	$ 7,014
Noncash expenses	U	922	922	922
Loan proceeds	V	-	-	14,000
Increase liabilities	W	700	680	(192)
Subtotal		$16,796	$18,760	$29,753
Less:				
Loan payments	X	$ 199	$ 201	$ 202
Purchase of assets	Y	8,000	8,000	8,000
Increase assets	Z	2,625	2,550	(720)
Subtotal		$10,824	$10,751	$ 7,482
Cash, ending balance		$ 5,972	$ 8,009	$22,271

On-Line Consultants, Inc.
Cash Flow Projection

Description	Apr	May	Jun
Cash, beginning balance	$22,271	$11,645	$11,549
Plus:			
Net profit	$12,135	$ 7,705	$ 9,200
Noncash expenses	922	922	922
Loan proceeds	-	-	-
Increase liabilities	352	-	422
Subtotal	$35,680	$20,272	$22,093
Less:			
Loan payments	$ 715	$ 723	$ 731
Purchase of assets	22,000	8,000	8,000
Increase assets	1,320	-	1,583
Subtotal	$24,035	$ 8,723	$10,314
Cash, ending balance	$11,645	$11,549	$11,779

On-Line Consultants, Inc.

ASSUMPTIONS

A: Gross Sales

Revenues are forecast based on existing contracts, expected renewals, and a reasonable estimate of new contracts.

Based on historical information, it is assumed that:
  a. Average monthly revenues over the past six months will continue at the same rates through the current contract term.
  b. All major accounts will renew their contracts at an average of 80% of existing revenue levels.

New contract revenues are calculated based on the firm's marketing referral plan. During the previous four six-month periods, we have retained no fewer than four new accounts per period. On average, three of these have remained with the firm for one year or more. Our forecast assumes three new clients during the six-month period. Historically, new accounts generate revenues averaging $3,400 per month.

1. Existing contracts

Account	Average monthly revenue	Months left on contract
Hanson and Company	$13,500	11
MPB Corporation	8,650	6
Abrams and Kemp	4,000	15
Brownstein Company	8,200	3
Dodge and Hockett	6,450	5
Taylor Corporation	4,800	2

2. Expected renewals

Account	Month	80% Average
Taylor Corporation	Mar	$ 3,840

Brownstein Company	Apr	6,560
Dodge and Hockett	Jun	5,160

3. New contracts

	Estimated month	Average amount
	Feb	$ 3,400
	Apr	3,400
	Jun	3,400

Worksheet

Account	Jan	Feb	Mar	Apr	May	Jun
Hanson	13,500	13,500	13,500	13,500	13,500	13,500
MPB Corporation	8,650	8,650	8,650	8,650	8,650	8,650
Abrams and Kemp	4,000	4,000	4,000	4,000	4,000	4,000
Brownstein:						
existing	8,200	8,200	8,200			
renewal				6,560	6,560	6,560
Dodge/Hockett:						
existing	6,450·	6,450	6,450	6,450	6,450	
renewal						5,160
Taylor Corp:						
existing	4,800	4,800				
renewal			3,840	3,840	3,840	3,840
New account #1		3,400	3,400	3,400	3,400	3,400
New account #2				3,400	3,400	3,400
New account #3						3,400
Total	45,600	49,000	48,040	49,800	49,800	51,910

B: Salaries and Wages

Current payroll includes seven employees and we are budgeting for two additional staff members to be hired in March and May.

Three employees are scheduled for annual reviews during the coming six months. It is assumed, based on advice from the president, that each will receive a salary increase of 10%.

Title	Current salary	Revision month
President	$4,000	
Vice president	3,750	
Account executive	3,200	March
Account executive	3,200	May
Account executive	3,200	
Office manager	2,100	June
Clerical	1,800	
Account executive	0	March ($2,800)
Account executive	0	May ($2,800)

Budget

Jan	$ 21,250
Feb	21,250
Mar	24,370
Apr	24,370
May	27,490
Jun	27,700
Total	$146,430

C: Payroll Taxes

Total payroll taxes, including federal and state, average 11.3% of payroll per month. No reduction is budgeted during this period.

Budget:

Jan	$ 2,401
Feb	2,401
Mar	2,754
Apr	2,754
May	3,106
Jun	3,130

D. Employee Benefits

The company provides group health insurance ($118 per person per month), and group life and disability insurance ($16 per $1,000 of payroll). No increases in rates are anticipated during this period.

Budget

	1	2	Total
Jan	$ 826	$ 336	$1,162
Feb	826	336	1,162
Mar	944	384	1,328
Apr	944	384	1,328
May	1,062	432	1,494
Jun	1,062	448	1,510
Total	$5,664	$2,320	$7,984

1—Group health insurance
2—Group life and disability insurance

E: Travel and Entertainment

The president and vice president are scheduled to attend a convention in New Orleans in February, at a cost of $2,200 each.

Account executives have a monthly auto and transportation allowance of $125.

Entertainment expenses average:
    $175 per month—president
    $118 per month—vice president
    $144 per month—account executives

It is suggested that with preapproval procedures in place, it will be possible to reduce average entertainment expenses for all account executives to $100 per month. The budget was prepared based on this assumption. ($175, president; $118, vice president; $100, all others.)

Budget

	1	2	3	Total
Jan	$	$ 375	$ 393	$ 768
Feb	4,400	375	393	5,168
Mar		500	493	993
Apr		500	493	993
May		625	593	1,218
Jun		625	593	1,218
Total	$4,400	$3,000	$2,958	$10,358

1—travel
2—transportation
3—entertainment

F: Advertising

The firm currently advertises each month in Data Professional magazine. The cost has been $318 per ad; however, we anticipate a 4% increase, budgeted in April.

Budget

Jan	$ 318
Feb	318
Mar	318
Apr	331
May	331
Jun	331
Total	$1,947

G: Printing

Expenses in this account include business cards, stationery, and internal forms.

We anticipate two business card orders (for new account executives) during the period. Current stationery inventory represents a ten-month supply, and no reorders are expected during the six months. Internal forms printing averages $24 per month.

Budget

	1	2	Total
Jan	$	$ 24	$ 24
Feb		24	24
Mar	36	24	60
Apr		24	24
May	36	24	60
Jun		24	24
Total	$ 72	$ 144	$ 216

1—business cards
2—internal forms

H: Office Supplies

This budget is based upon average costs of $59.90 per employee. Three years ago, averages were $45 per employee. This average has been adjusted 10% per year, in line with increases in supply costs.

Recent averages per employee have run $64.50. It is suggested that centralizing supply purchases through the office manager will help reduce per-employee costs, to $59.90 each per month:

Budget

	Employees	Budget
Jan	7	$ 419
Feb	7	419
Mar	8	479
Apr	8	479
May	9	539
Jun	9	539
Total		$2,874

I: Interest Expense

The company is paying on an existing loan granted in December. The balance is $16,000 at 11.5%. Payments are due to continue over five years. The amortization schedule for the next six months is:

Month	Total	Interest	Principal	Balance
				$16,000
Jan	$ 352	$ 153	$ 199	15,801
Feb	352	151	201	15,600
Mar	352	150	202	15,398
Apr	352	148	204	15,194
May	352	146	206	14,988
Jun	352	144	208	14,780
Total interest		$ 892		
Total principal (See ref. X)			$1,220	

The firm anticipates applying for an additional $14,000 loan to acquire new office furniture during the six-month period. It is assumed the loan will be granted at 13.5% interest, and will be scheduled for a 24-month repayment period. We expect to obtain the loan during March, with payments to begin in April:

Month	Total	Interest	Principal	Balance
				$14,000
Apr	$ 669	$ 158	$ 511	13,489
May	669	152	517	12,972
Jun	669	146	523	12,449
Total interest		$ 456		
Total principal (See ref. X)			$1,551	

Budget

Jan	$ 153
Feb	151
Mar	150
Apr	306
May	298
Jun	290
Total	$1,348

J: Rent

The current lease calls for monthly payments of $1,150. No increases are scheduled during the period. (See also ref. N)

Budget

Jan	$1,150
Feb	1,150
Mar	1,150
Apr	1,150
May	1,150
Jun	1,150
Total	$6,900

K: Postage and Delivery

During the past year, postage has averaged $206 per month. No significant changes have occurred from one month to another, and no postal rate increases are expected in the near future.

Delivery charges have averaged $183 per month, a substantial portion for overnight express charges. It is suggested that with preapproval of overnight delivery, we will be able to reduce this expense to $110 per month.

Budget

	1	2	Total
Jan	$ 206	$ 110	$ 316
Feb	206	110	316
Mar	206	110	316
Apr	206	110	316
May	206	110	316
Jun	206	110	316
Total	$1,236	$ 660	$1,896

L: Dues and Subscriptions

Current expenses include membership in one national association, with the annual renewal dues scheduled for payment in May; and subscriptions to seven magazines. Three of these are scheduled for renewal during the coming six-month period. The president wants to renew all subscriptions.

Budget

	M	S	Total
Jan	$	$	$
Feb		35	35
Mar			
Apr		42	42
May	250	18	268
Jun			
Total	$250	$ 95	$345

M: Equipment Leases

The firm currently leases a postage meter ($63 per month) and one computer terminal ($416 per month). Both leases run beyond the six-month period, and no increases are anticipated in this account.

Budget

Jan	$ 479
Feb	479
Mar	479
Apr	479
May	479
Jun	479
Total	$2,874

N: Telephone and Utilities

Telephone charges have averaged $835 per month over the past year. All clients of the firm are within the state, and no significant increase in toll calls is expected in the future. The telephone company has requested an 8% rate increase, and it should be assumed that this will be approved. We have included an increase starting in April.

The firm pays its own electric bill as part of its rent agreement (see ref. J). Average billings during the Jan–Mar period are expected to run $285 per month; and during the Apr–Jun period, $194 per month. These estimates are based upon average payments during the last three years.

Budget

	1	2	Total
Jan	$ 835	$ 285	$1,120
Feb	835	285	1,120
Mar	835	285	1,120
Apr	902	194	1,096
May	902	194	1,096
Jun	902	194	1,096
Total	$5,211	$1,437	$6,648

1—telephone
2—utilities

O: Repairs and Maintenance

All anticipated expenses in this account are expected to occur under coverage provided in yearly maintenance contracts. During the six-month period, two annual payments are due:

Equipment	Amount	Due
Computer hardware	$1,235	Jan
Two electric typewriters	216	Mar

Budget

Jan	$1,235
Feb	
Mar	216
Apr	
May	
Jun	
Total	$1,451

P: Insurance

The firm's comprehensive insurance policy premium was paid for one full year in October. We are amortizing 1/12th of the total premium of $3,616 during each month (see ref. U).

Worker's compensation insurance averages 27 cents per $100 of payroll, adjusted to 88% of that amount for a favorable experience modification (average 23.76 cents per $100 of payroll). This is accrued each month.

Budget

	1	2	Total
Jan	$ 301	$ 50	$ 351
Feb	301	50	351
Mar	301	58	359
Apr	301	58	359
May	301	65	366
Jun	301	66	367
Total	$1,806	$347	$2,153

1—amortization of prepaid insurance
2—worker's compensation accrual

Q: Legal and Professional Fees

The firm's annual audit has been quoted at $4,200, and will be payable in March. No additional accounting or auditing fees are expected during the period.

No increase and no additional fees are budgeted.

Budget

	A	L	Total
Jan	$	800	$ 800
Feb		800	800
Mar	4,200	800	5,000
Apr		800	800
May		800	800
June		800	800
Total	$4,200	$4,800	$9,000

R: Depreciation

Our estimate of total depreciation to be claimed during the year is $7,450, including an allowance for assets we intend to acquire. This is budgeted evenly throughout the period, with one-half the annual total attributable to this period.

Budget

Jan	$ 621
Feb	621
Mar	621
Apr	621
May	621
Jun	621
Total	$3,726

S: Miscellaneous

This account has averaged $113 per month during the past year. With improved coding procedures in place, it is estimated that expenses charged here can be reduced to $75 per month.

Budget

Jan	$ 75
Feb	75
Mar	75
Apr	75
May	75
Jun	75
Total	$450

T: Provision for Taxes

The liability for federal income taxes is calculated on the assumption that current rates will remain in effect for the entire year. Total profits are estimated for the six-month period at $71,000, and should be taxed as follows:

$$\$50,000 \times 15\% = \$ \ 7,500$$
$$\$21,000 \times 25\% = \ \ 5,250$$
$$\text{Total} \quad \$12,750$$

Budget

Jan	$ 1,944
Feb	1,974
Mar	1,238
Apr	2,142
May	2,388
Jun	3,064
Total	$12,750

U: Noncash Expenses

This adjustment consists of:
1. Depreciation allowance, which is a noncash journal entry made each month.
2. Insurance amortization for annual premium paid in October, $301 entry each month (see ref. P).

Several other expense accounts contain monthly or quarterly accruals that are considered minor and, accordingly, are not adjusted from one month to the next.

Projection

	D	I	Total
Jan	$ 621	$ 301	$ 922
Feb	$ 621	$ 301	$ 922
Mar	$ 621	$ 301	$ 922
Apr	$ 621	$ 301	$ 922
May	$ 621	$ 301	$ 922
Jun	$ 621	$ 301	$ 922
Total	$3,726	$1,806	$5,532

V: Loan Proceeds

The firm will apply for a loan of $14,000 in March, to purchase new office furniture.

Projection

Jan	$
Feb	
Mar	14,000
Apr	
May	
Jun	
Total	$14,000

W: Increase in Liabilities

It is anticipated that liability balances will increase during the six-month period by 20% of the monthly growth in gross income. This estimate is based on historical averages over the last three years.

Projection

Jan	$ 700
Feb	680
Mar	(192)
Apr	352
May	
Jun	422
Total	$1,962

X: Loan Proceeds

The principal portion of notes payable consists of:
1. An existing loan for $16,000, payable over five years at 11.5%.
2. A new loan with payments expected to begin in April, for $14,000, payable over two years at 13.5% interest.

Also see ref. I.

Projection

	Existing Loan	New Loan	Total
Jan	$ 199	$	$ 199
Feb	201		201
Mar	202		202
Apr	204	511	715
May	206	517	723
Jun	208	523	731
Total	$1,220	$1,551	$2,771

Y: Purchase of Assets

The firm anticipates using $14,000 loan proceeds received in March to purchase new office furniture in April.

We will continue to deposit $8,000 per month with the current owner of the building we occupy, as part of our existing lease-purchase agreement.

Projection

	1	2	Total
Jan	$	$ 8,000	$ 8,000
Feb		8,000	8,000
Mar		8,000	8,000
Apr	14,000	8,000	22,000
May		8,000	8,000
Jun		8,000	8,000
Total	$14,000	$48,000	$62,000

1—purchase office furniture
2—deposit on lease-purchase

Z: Increase in Assets

Accounts receivable balances are expected to increase by 75% of monthly increases in revenue, based upon historical averages.

Projection

Jan	$2,625
Feb	2,550
Mar	(720)
Apr	1,320
May	
Jun	1,583
Total	$7,358

Index

A

Account analysis, 89
Accounting for variances, 98–99
  revision requests and, 98
  revisions as a result of, 98
  rolling budgets and, 98–99
Accounts receivable, 93
Acting on the budget, 87–88
Anticipating budget questions, 69
Anticipating future problems, 81
Applications of funds, 52
Arbitrary changes, 108–109
Assumption
  base, 26–30
  cash flow worksheet for, 55
  complex, 68–69
  defined, 14
  developing the, 51–58
  elements of, 38–39
  flawed, 43
  incorrect, 22
  original, 97
  poor, 81
  researching, 22
  testing, 30–31, 43–44
  validity of, 45
Assumption base, *defined*, 14
Attitudes, 121–122
Authority for budgeting, 113–114

B

Backward budgeting, 24
Balance Sheet, 52
Believing bigger is better, 109–110
Blaming or distorting, 10–11
  and management pressure, 10
  and political conflict, 10
  instead of solving, 10
Budget
  above last year, 106–107
  acting on, 87–88
  anticipating questions of, 69
  backward, 24
  defined, 14
  expense base, 34–43